PREDICTING
— YOUR —
FUTURE

ITALIAN TAROT CARD,
"THE WORLD," BY ANTONIO
CICOGNARA, 16TH CENTURY

DK PUBLISHING, INC.

A CHINESE GROUP STUDIES
THE YIN AND YANG
SYMBOL, 17TH CENTURY

For Edith Pettigrew, with love

A DK PUBLISHING BOOK
www.dk.com

Project Editor • Tracie Lee Davis
Art Editor • Anna Benjamin
Senior Editor • Sharon Lucas
Senior Art Editor • Tim Scott
Managing Editor • Francis Ritter
Managing Art Editor • Derek Coombes
DTP Designer • Sonia Charbonnier
Picture Researcher • Andy Sansom
Production • Ruth Charlton, Wendy Penn

First American Edition, 1999

2 4 6 8 10 9 7 5 3 1

Published in the United States by DK Publishing, Inc., 95 Madison Avenue, New York, New York 10016
Copyright © 1999 Dorling Kindersley Limited • Text copyright © 1999 Julia and Derek Parker

DK Publishing books are available at special discounts for bulk purchases for sales promotions or premiums.
Special editions, including personalized covers, excerpts of existing guides, and corporate imprints can be created in large quantities for specific needs.
For more information, contact Special Markets Dept./DK Publishing, Inc./95 Madison Ave./New York, NY 10016/Fax: 800-600-9098.

Library of Congress Cataloging-in-Publication Data
Parker, Derek.
    Parkers' prediction pack : a compelling guide to divination : look
into the future and plan your life using three systems of
prediction--I ching, tarot, runes. -- 1st American ed.
        p. cm. -- (DK millennium)
Written by Derek Parker and Julia Parker.
    ISBN 0-7894-4611-1 (alk. paper)
    1. Fortune-telling.   2. Divination.   I. Parker, Julia
II. Title.   III. Series.
BF1861.P365   1999
133.3--dc21   99-30470
                                                                CIP

Predicting Your Future printed by Wing King Tong Co. Ltd, Hong Kong
Divination Chooser Wheel, Instructions, Rune Sheet, and *Box* printed and assembled by New Island Printing Co. Ltd, China
Tarot Cards produced by Fournier, Spain • *I Ching Coins* manufactured by Westair Reproductions Ltd, UK

CONTENTS

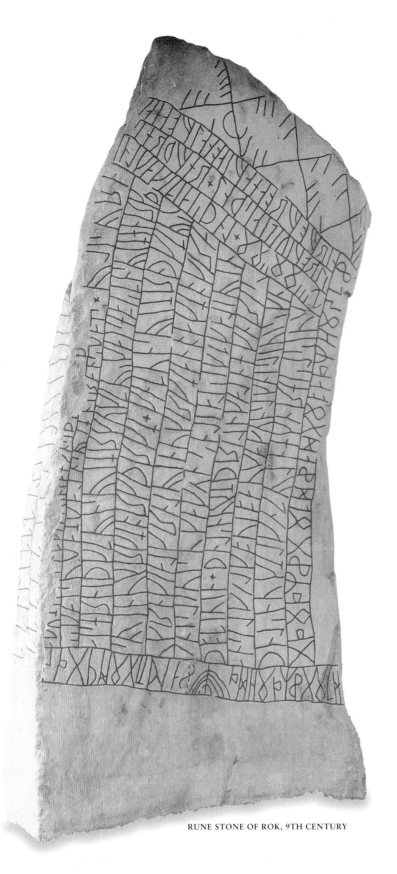

RUNE STONE OF ROK, 9TH CENTURY

Introduction 4

TAROT 6
The Tarot Spreads 8
The Major Arcana 10
The Minor Arcana 18
Cups 20
Wands 22
Pentacles 24
Swords 26
Tarot – A Case History 28

RUNES 30
The Rune Castings 32
Frey's Aett 34
Hagal's Aett 36
Tyr's Aett 38
Runes – A Case History 40

I CHING 42
Consulting the I Ching 44
The Hexagrams 46
I Ching – Two Case Histories 78

Acknowledgments 80

INTRODUCTION

MOST PEOPLE BELIEVE THAT WE CANNOT MAKE THE STATEMENT "THIS WILL HAPPEN" WITH REAL CONFIDENCE. TAKE PERHAPS THE MOST DEPENDABLE PREDICTION WE CAN MAKE: THAT THE SUN WILL RISE TOMORROW MORNING. EVEN THIS IS UNCERTAIN: ONE DAY THE SUN WILL EXPAND AND BURN EARTH TO A CINDER; THERE WILL BE NO SUN TO RISE OR EARTH FOR IT TO SHINE UPON.

SIMPLER PREDICTIONS ARE EQUALLY FALLIBLE. WE SAY "Tomorrow morning I shall have coffee for breakfast," or "I'm staying in this evening and watching television." But we know perfectly well that all kinds of things may happen to interfere with our plans. Professional forecasters of the weather or of stock exchange movements are no more dependable.

Irrationally, we often have more confidence in predictions that are even less sure, such as "I will win the lottery this week," or "He/she will love me," or "I'll get a promotion this year." We tend to believe these because we want them to be true. But is it possible to know the future simply because we want to? Can the Tarot or the *I Ching* or the runes predict the future any more accurately than we can ourselves? The answer depends on our notion of time; and time is a mysterious concept, about which there are many questions to be asked.

Fifteen hundred years ago, St. Augustine said, "I know what time is, as long as no one asks me to explain it. If I want to explain it to someone, then I don't know." The situation hasn't changed much, despite the attempts of philosophers and scientists to tell us what time is – or whether indeed it exists at all. Time depends on our measurement of it, whether by weeks, days, hours, minutes, or seconds. If there were no one in the universe to count the passing of time, would time exist?

Aztec Calendar Stone

Ever since the passing of time has been recorded, the future has been predicted. This Aztec Calendar stone predicts the world will end in an earthquake.

OUR CONCEPTION OF TIME

The existence of time is a vital question where predicting the future is concerned. If there were no such thing as time until humankind invented it, then it is conceivable that we may have got it wrong. We tend to think of time as a piece of string with a knot in it. The present, where we are, is the knot; on one side of the knot the string stretches back into the past; and on the the other side of the knot the string stretches forward into the future.

I Ching Consultation

Chinese priests tossed stalks made of bamboo, as shown here, or yarrow, to consult the wisdom of the I Ching.

Early Tarot
This 16th-century card is from Le Monde Primitif pack, one of the earliest designed for divinatory purposes.

But maybe time is more like a CD, with its invisible grooves. Maybe we can move around it just as the laser beam can move to and fro across the disc, at one moment playing track 14, but capable in another moment of moving back to track 2 (in the past) or on to track 20 (in the future). If this is so, all we have to learn is how to move the laser.

SYNCHRONICITY

For as long as we have looked into the past, humans have attempted to see the shape of things to come. Few people today predict the future by capnomancy (reading the smoke from burning poppy leaves), ichthyomancy (examining the entrails of fish), or onychomancy (looking at the patterns of oil on the fingernails of a male virgin). But the Tarot, the runes, and the *I Ching* have survived for countless centuries. The main theory of forecasting by using this pack is related to the idea of synchronicity, a term invented by the great 20th-century psychologist C. G. Jung. Like the ancient Chinese, Jung believed that anything that happens is related to everything else that happens, during the time when the happening occurs. According to synchronicity, at the very moment you decide to ask a question about the future, future happenings are related to your action in throwing down the coins or picking up the cards or runes. One has a bearing on the other.

CONFIDENCE AND CREATIVITY

The main element in using the three methods of prediction in this pack is probably confidence. Just as one doubter in a room can upset the atmosphere enough to make hypnosis difficult or impossible, so attempting to read the Tarot, cast the runes, or consult the *I Ching* without truly believing that one can gain something from the exercise will be fruitless. There is absolutely no point in using these disciplines flippantly; and indeed it may be that such an attitude is actually dangerous. Be respectful, and do not treat them as playthings.

An important element in all divination is imagination. Each rune or card or hexagram has a traditional meaning, but, like the seer's crystal ball, they are also meant to focus your mind on the question you are asking – they are both medium and message. There must be a creative input from the "reader."

Which particular method of prediction you use is a matter for you. Some will be drawn to the ancient trigrams and hexagrams of the *I Ching*, some to the decorative and highly mythical Tarot, others to the Nordic simplicity of the runes. It does seem, however, that each of these systems tends to be better applied to particular problems or areas of life; and in the Divination Chooser Wheel you will discover our suggestions as to which discipline you might apply to various queries. When using any of the three divination systems, be decisive, be brave, be confident. If the past exists, so does the future. Take the next step toward it.

Frankish Casket
Scenes of Christian and Germanic tradition on this 8th-century whalebone casket are surrounded by runic script.

TAROT

THERE HAVE BEEN MANY THEORIES ABOUT THE ORIGIN OF TAROT CARDS, WHICH HAVE BEEN USED BOTH FOR DIVINATION AND CARD GAMES. IT HAS BEEN SUGGESTED THAT THEY ORIGINATED THOUSANDS OF YEARS AGO, BUT ALL THAT IS KNOWN FOR CERTAIN IS THAT THEY APPEARED IN THEIR PRESENT FORM IN ITALY AND FRANCE IN THE LATE 14TH CENTURY.

The Page of Pentacles

The images of the traditional Tarot packs that we are familiar with today originated in the early Renaissance period. This card is from a late-15th century pack attributed to Italian artist Antonio di Cicognara.

THE SYMBOLS OF THE SWORD, CUP, AND BATON THAT APPEAR ON THREE OF THE FOUR SUITS OF THE TAROT PACK ARE SOMETIMES SHOWN IN THE hands of Hindu statues, which suggests India as a possible birthplace for Tarot, or they may have been brought to Italy by the explorer Marco Polo during his travels to and from China. The association with the gypsies is probably mistaken, because Tarot packs were known in Europe earlier than when the gypsies were supposed to have brought them from Arabia. Tarot cards were initially used for playing games, although the gypsies always seem to have used them for fortunetelling. They appeared in Italy in 1299, and had spread to Spain by 1371. They reached Germany and probably France by 1380 (King Charles VI is known to have bought three packs in 1392), and they were selling well in England by 1465. Columbus seems to have taken a pack to the Americas, but Tarot cards were mainly used for gaming. It is only comparatively recently – from the middle of the 18th century – that they have been considered particularly mysterious and occult. By then, the conventional packs that are now used for card games had evolved from the Tarot pack – with the four suits of hearts, diamonds, clubs, and spades.

THE TAROT PACK

The Tarot packs we use today are of various designs. The traditional packs are based on 14th-century Venetian or Piedmontese designs. They consist of 78 cards divided into two groups, the Major Arcana, which has 22 cards, and the Minor Arcana, consisting of the remaining 56 cards. The Major Arcana cards carry pictures representing various characteristics or archetypes, and are numbered I to XXI, with the Fool unnumbered. The cards of the Minor Arcana consist of four suits of 14 cards each, which are very like the suits of ordinary playing cards – with hearts called cups; clubs called wands, batons, or rods; diamonds called pentacles, coins, or disks; and spades called swords. There are four court cards in each suit, and ten numbered cards.

There are a wide variety of Tarot pack designs available today, from ones that reproduce early historical illustrations to modern versions that bear little resemblance to the familiar images of the Tarot. There are Tarot packs bearing symbolism from different cultures, such as the Native American Tarot and the Kashmir Tarot. Astrology is commonly

Divining the Future
The Tarot pack was originally used to play a card game called "Tarot" in France and "Tarocco" in Italy. It was only during the 18th century that divination with Tarot cards was practiced seriously.

linked to Tarot, and some card designs incorporate astrological symbols alongside the Tarot symbols. Because the messages in the cards are universal, meanings are not likely to be lost when packs are illustrated to appeal to different readers. For the *Parkers' Prediction Pack* we have chosen to use a popular European pack, the Spanish Tarot (*see right*), based on a traditional design originally created in 1736.

USING THE CARDS

Treat your Tarot cards with respect, and do not lend them to anyone. When you remove your cards from this pack, wrap them in a piece of silk, then store them in a box – preferably a wooden one. Familiarize yourself with the illustrations. Some of the number cards can be difficult to read, and it is hard to know whether some of them are inverted or not. You might like to pencil an arrow on the back of each card, pointing to its top. An inverted card is one that appears upside down when the cards are spread. If a card is inverted, it suggests that its problematic aspects might come to the fore.

Choose a spread suitable to the question you wish to ask the cards (*see page 8*). If you are reading the Tarot for someone else, give the pack to your subject (the querent) to shuffle and cut three times, or swirl them clockwise on a flat surface. The inquirer must then select the cards and hand them to you, face down, in turn. Place them in the order and arrangement shown in the diagrams. When the spread is complete, turn the card over sideways, not top to bottom. Take care to follow the order of the layout shown in the diagrams.

THE TAROT SPREADS

BEFORE YOU READ THE TAROT, YOU NEED TO ESTABLISH WHICH SPREAD YOU WILL USE. EACH SPREAD IS PARTICULARLY SUITABLE FOR A CERTAIN TYPE OF QUESTION. ONCE YOU KNOW THE QUESTION, YOU CAN CHOOSE THE MOST APPROPRIATE SPREAD, SELECT THE CORRECT NUMBER OF CARDS, AND LAY THEM IN THE ORDER SHOWN IN ONE OF THE SPREADS ON THESE TWO PAGES.

THE PYRAMID SPREAD

The Pyramid spread is a classic. It should only be used when you need direction in life or are about to make important changes. Do not use this spread too often – if you do, both you and the cards may become confused, and it is unlikely that you will get a clear picture of your situation and of the way ahead. Use this spread only two or three times a year – perhaps when you believe you have reached a crossroads in your life, or are presented with a particularly difficult problem or situation and need special guidance. Pay close attention to the blocks of cards, and remember that cards 1–4 focus on the past, 5–8 on the present, and so on. Study the Major Arcana cards carefully: their wise messages and the questions they ask you are crucial. The court cards, too, will vividly represent the people involved with you and your situation.

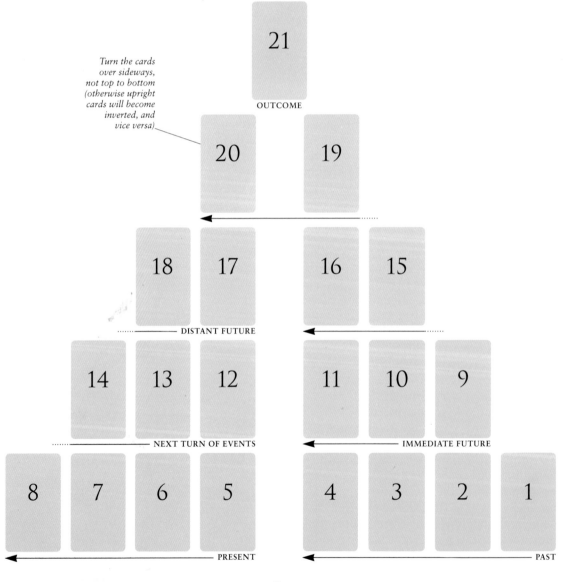

Turn the cards over sideways, not top to bottom (otherwise upright cards will become inverted, and vice versa)

21 OUTCOME

20   19

18   17   16   15
DISTANT FUTURE

14   13   12   11   10   9
NEXT TURN OF EVENTS   IMMEDIATE FUTURE

8   7   6   5   4   3   2   1
PRESENT   PAST

THE YES/NO SPREAD

The Yes/No is a simple spread that can be used when you need a little help in arriving at a day-to-day decision. Deal the Tarot cards face down as below. Turn the cards over once they are all laid out. The result is based on a points system. If a card is the right way up, it receives one point. If a card is inverted (upside down), no points are awarded. Card number 3 is a key card, and if it is the correct way up it receives two points. If the majority of cards are the right way, up the answer is yes; if inverted, the answer is no. Count the points. If the total is an even number, the cards are undecided.

Place cards in the order as numbered

5   4   3   2   1

THE ZODIAC SPREAD

The relationship between astrology and Tarot is strong: astrological symbols appear in some Tarot decks, and many Tarot cards have associations with the planets, and the signs of the zodiac. The Zodiac spread is suitable for occasional use: perhaps for an assessment of the present situation, or when you wish to learn more about yourself, and your reactions and motivations. The placing of the cards derives from the circle of the horoscope. Place 12 Tarot cards in a circle, starting from the 9 o'clock position (number 1 in the diagram), and continue to place the cards counterclockwise. Carefully interpret each card in relation to the sphere of life represented by the 12 "houses" of the horoscope.

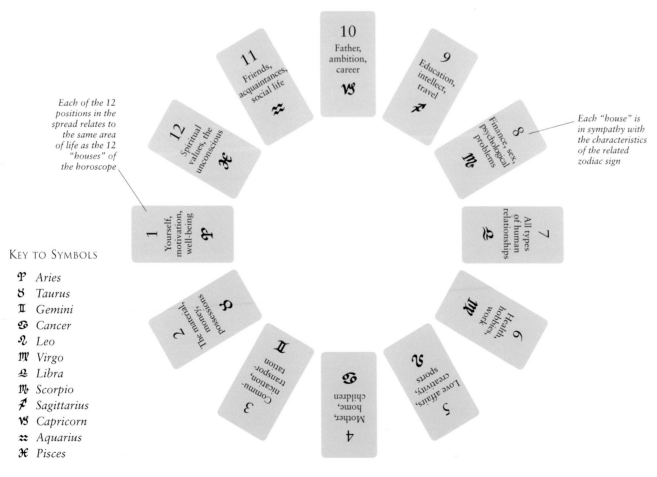

Each of the 12 positions in the spread relates to the same area of life as the 12 "houses" of the horoscope

Each "house" is in sympathy with the characteristics of the related zodiac sign

10 Father, ambition, career ♑

11 Friends, acquaintances, social life ♒

9 Education, intellect, travel ♐

12 Spiritual values, the unconscious ♓

8 Finance, sex, psychological problems ♏

1 Yourself, motivation, well-being ♈

7 All types of human relationships ♎

2 The material, money, possessions ♉

6 Health, work, hobbies ♍

3 Communication, transportation ♊

5 Love affairs, creativity, sports ♌

4 Mother, home, children ♋

KEY TO SYMBOLS

♈ *Aries*
♉ *Taurus*
♊ *Gemini*
♋ *Cancer*
♌ *Leo*
♍ *Virgo*
♎ *Libra*
♏ *Scorpio*
♐ *Sagittarius*
♑ *Capricorn*
♒ *Aquarius*
♓ *Pisces*

THE MAJOR ARCANA

The standard Tarot deck consists of 78 cards in total, split into two parts: 22 cards known as the Major Arcana are the heart of the Tarot deck, while the rest of the cards are known as the Minor Arcana. The 22 cards of the Major Arcana are the most interesting of the Tarot, representing every condition of human life and offering advice and assistance.

Each of the cards in the Major Arcana represents an aspect of universal human experience. Each card also has a name that either directly conveys the meaning of the card, such as Strength or Justice, or depicts individuals, such as the Hermit or the Empress, that represent human archetypes. These archetypes symbolize qualities that are universally understood. The Hermit, for instance, represents solitude and the wisdom that is associated with old age. Each card is numbered, apart from the Fool, which is often considered to be the querent – the person setting out on the journey of inquiry.

THE CARDS' MEANING
Because each card symbolizes an element of human experience or depicts a human archetype, their messages are meaningful and apt and can easily be interpreted by

everyone who uses them. While the cards have universal meanings, each person brings their own personal interpretation to them. Each card will be read in a different way depending on who is reading it and what question they are asking. For one querent the Hermit might be advising a period of solitude and a time for self-reflection, while for another he could symbolize that it is time to return to the hurly-burly of life and the pursuit of knowledge after a period of spiritual renewal.

LISTENING TO THE CARDS
When a card of the Major Arcana appears in a spread, it is usually given greater weight than Minor Arcana cards. Cards of the Major Arcana draw emphasis to a specific aspect of our lives. They make suggestions, sometimes hinting very broadly, but they can never make up our minds for us. We

must choose our own destiny. The cards can also help us deal with the past by coming to terms with what was negative, putting it behind us and moving forward. We cannot change the past, we can only accept it – by bringing the hidden out into the open we clear our inhibitions, enabling us to move on freely and become more positive in outlook. The cards help us to consider the way ahead: does the future look bright – or is it stormy? They try to prepare us for what is going to happen and show us how we can achieve what we desire, as well as how to cope if the immediate outlook is less positive.

The wisdom of the Tarot is age-old. The more you use it, the more this will become apparent to you and the more you will respect it. The Tarot has survived for hundreds of years, and what it has to say is as relevant today as it has always been.

THE FOOL

This unnumbered card depicts a man – often considered to represent the querent – setting out on a journey. He carries a bundle that may contain provisions for the journey, or may represent his burdens in life. He is supported by a strong staff; but he is not looking directly ahead, and there is uncertainty in his expression. A little dog (in some Tarot packs a cat) tears at his breeches. The dog may be accompanying the Fool on his journey. Alternatively, he may be trying to prevent him from leaving home, suggesting that the journey might be a mistake.

What the Fool is telling you
The Fool is telling you to listen to your wiser self, and to think carefully before making any move. He reminds you that a thoughtless

action will inhibit your progress. He suggests that you should develop a sense of purpose and not allow yourself to become hesitant and indecisive. He says you may well be at the beginning of a new and important project, in which case you must prepare the ground very thoroughly and make certain that you see every aspect of your present situation clearly and with a calm, resolute mind.

Questions to ask yourself
Am I prepared intellectually and physically for what lies ahead? Is my judgment sound, or am I justifying my actions or evading important issues? Am I behaving immaturely or as a responsible adult? Am I enthusiastic or blindly optimistic about what lies ahead? Do I need to become more focused?

KEY WORDS
New beginnings, spontaneity, folly.

I THE MAGICIAN

The Magician stands at his table, displaying objects representing the four suits of the Minor Arcana. He seems to be saying, "This is what is on offer – take it, and use it to your advantage." He appears wise, but he is also artful and cunning. His sideways glance puts us on our guard. The brim of his hat represents the figure eight, which relates to occultism and to the Greek god Hermes – better known to us as Mercury, in astrology the ruling planet of Gemini and Virgo.

What the Magician is telling you

The Magician suggests that you should be more aware of your weaknesses – self-awareness is an important element of psychological wholeness. Do not rush into decisions: impulsiveness may cause trouble in the future. However difficult the situation in which you find yourself, be calm and practical. Discretion is vital. Do not try to be too clever or cunning. Be truthful and direct, and do not be afraid to take a firm, positive line of action. You are in a position to influence others now and in the long term. Your originality and compassion are heightened at the moment, though you may be unnecessarily tense or worried. Perhaps you need to spend more time relaxing.

Questions to ask yourself

Am I avoiding important issues? Am I being deceptive? Am I currently trying to talk my way out of a difficult situation? Is my approach practical enough? Am I facing up to reality? Am I being entirely honest with myself?

KEY WORDS
Skill, adaptability, duplicity.

II THE HIGH PRIESTESS

THE HIGH PRIESTESS

KEY WORDS
Intuition, inner calm, patience.

The High Priestess, or female Pope, as she is sometimes described, always sits with an open book on her lap. She appears quietly confident and challenges masculine authority. Wise and formidable, she is in control not only of what is going on around her, but of her own emotions. She is sympathetic to the zodiac sign Virgo.

What the High Priestess is telling you

If you are a woman: Be confident in your approach to life, its problems, and what it has to offer. You are far stronger than you may realize, but must avoid overbearing behavior. To be at your best, think before you speak and make sure of your ground before you commit yourself verbally or on paper. Aim for higher study and knowledge.

If you are a man: Become more aware of your feminine side, and allow yourself a freer flow of emotion. Listen to your intuition; it could be a greater help than you realize. With both sexes, the High Priestess asks you to consider your health and physical well-being.

Questions to ask yourself

Women: Am I worrying unnecessarily? Am I trying to do too much? Do I get minor problems out of perspective? Do I need to relax more? Would I enjoy some kind of challenging study? Men: Am I being too macho? Do I put down women? Am I in too much of a hurry? Both sexes: Am I as fit as I should be, or should I exercise more? Is worry affecting my health? Do I get bogged down with detail and fail to take a broad enough look at life?

III THE EMPRESS

The Empress is pictured sitting on a throne. She represents an archetypal female – a matriarchal figure. She enjoys all the good things of life and bestows them on those she loves. She is sensual, but needs both emotional and financial security. She brings harmony into relationships. In her role as the Emperor's consort she is the power behind the throne, although she does not appear to dominate her male partner. Her powers lie in the female domain. She relates very closely to the zodiac sign Taurus and its ruling planet Venus.

What the Empress is telling you

The Empress encourages you to enjoy material comfort and sexual fulfillment, but to avoid overindulgence. She says that your financial position will improve, but tells you to be circumspect and to do everything you can to increase your money in a safe way (she never encourages risk-taking). Under her influence, business partnerships will flourish. Harmony in your life will increase at this time, and with it will come emotional security. If you are feeling ready to start a family, she indicates that now would be a good time to do so, for she has some bearing on procreation.

Questions to ask yourself

Am I being sensible where money is concerned? Is money too important to me? Should I get out more? Am I overeating? Am I overweight? Am I as forthcoming as I should be toward my partner, or am I being possessive or even jealous? Should I try to improve my sex life?

KEY WORDS
Security, pleasure, harmony.

IIII THE EMPEROR

The Emperor represents temporal power through the exploitation of energetic and assertive action. Tradition decrees that he has learned the hard way, having overcome anger and violent behavior. He has achieved everything he set out to do. With increasing age he has mellowed and gathered wisdom; yet he still has a great deal of fiery energy. He is the archetypal male, and is related to the zodiac sign Aries and its ruling planet Mars.

What the Emperor is telling you

He is giving you confidence and saying that success will come if you channel your energy and use it positively. He is old and wise, and has learned that premature action does not pay off – he warns you against it. He encourages you to be firm but not ruthless; assertive tendencies must be controlled. You must be patient when dealing with other people. The Emperor reminds you that being in a powerful position increases the amount of responsibility you carry. He encourages women to become assertive and independent. He suggests that we should expend spare energy on exercise.

Questions to ask yourself

Am I too pushy? Do I have a "me first" attitude that could harm those who love me? Is my nature so passionate that it rules my head? Am I being stubborn? Am I often aggressive in speech or action? Do I control my temper? Am I learning from past mistakes? Do I resort to immature behavior when I don't get my own way?

KEY WORDS
Action, energy, assertiveness.

V THE HIGH PRIEST

KEY WORDS
Spiritual development, learning.

The High Priest represents spiritual wisdom and is the mediator between heaven and earth. He is a great teacher, always compassionate and fair. A sympathetic ruler, he listens and is merciful. He has breadth of vision and is able to encompass and understand all the needs of man. He emphasizes the importance of learning and the role of the individual in society. The High Priest is related to the astrological influence of the planet Jupiter.

What the High Priest is telling you

He expects you to follow his example and to be merciful. He also insists that you adhere to the rules and set a good example for others. You must not become restless or bored when he confronts you with these qualities, or give up if you think that they are unattainable. He stresses that you choose for yourself and take your own path, knowing that learning through experience is the right way. He encourages you not to get bogged down with the detail of your present situation: it is best to take a broad view and to control every tendency toward blind optimism and over-enthusiasm. He wants you to be adventurous, but warns against taking unnecessary risks.

Questions to ask yourself

Am I being fair and just to other people? Do I give enough encouragement and help when and where it is needed? Do I ignore good advice when it is offered? Is there anything that I can do to make me a better, more compassionate human being? Am I really as broad-minded as I profess to be?

VI THE LOVERS

Here is a loving pair uniting in marriage. Cupid shoots arrows as they plight their troth. While they appear to represent all that is best in earthly love and happiness, some traditions assert that the pair represent virtue and vice – basic alternatives. Although their love is being energized by the sun, we must not forget that Cupid is hardly angelic – he inflames passion, which can easily become anger rather than love.

What the Lovers are telling you

The Lovers want you to be happy and enjoy your relationship. However, you must be prepared to compromise and to make sacrifices if it is to work successfully. They encourage you to maintain a sense of humor at all times and to keep jealousy at bay. Harmony will be enhanced by shared interests and aspirations. They warn you of undue rivalry with your loved one. Senseless bickering must be controlled; and even when things go wrong it is vital to keep calm. They warn you not to fall in love with love: it is the other person who matters, and it is important that you know his or her true character.

Questions to ask yourself

Am I being fair to my lover? Am I receptive to what he or she is thinking, wants to achieve or do? Am I jealous for no reason? Or, if I have cause, can I possibly talk things over in a civilized manner? Do I truly love him or her? Am I getting involved with this person merely because of wealth or status? Am I hurting my lover?

KEY WORDS
Love, harmony, choices, sacrifice.

VII THE CHARIOT

Here a handsome young man sets out on an adventure, or returns victorious from battle. His chariot is drawn by two horses (sometimes sphinxes) who offer him wisdom, but also represent his spiritual and sexual drives. He is powerful, demonstrated by his crown, and he is positive in outlook. He represents youth, achievement and popularity. The Chariot is related to the zodiac sign Sagittarius.

What the Chariot is telling you

The Chariot suggests that you are quite right to feel strong and optimistic. You should accept any challenge that is offered. Your enthusiasm will carry you through, and you are in an excellent position to encourage others to take part in your enterprise. The Chariot encourages you to expand your horizons through study and adventure. Whatever your age, you are young at heart. Success will come with self-awareness, hard work, and sheer determination. The time is right for travel, for intellectual journeys, and for fulfilling your potential. The Chariot's influence encourages you to study foreign languages and to consider other cultures.

Questions to ask yourself

Am I at a point in my life where I can develop my potential? Can I dispel any uncertainty that I am feeling? Who can I seek advice from? Or if you are about to start a new enterprise: Am I well-prepared for my challenge? Am I blindly optimistic? Can I cope with unforeseen developments? Do I have enough financial backing for my enterprise?

KEY WORDS
Challenge, travel, expansion.

VIII JUSTICE

KEY WORDS
Balance, restraint.

Justice strives to maintain the balance between positivity and negativity. She holds the scales and has the power to differentiate between right and wrong. Behind her throne there are sometimes depicted two upright columns representing moral strength and integrity. She can be stern but is always fair; and while her expression is serious, she is good at heart. Justice is related to the astrological influence of Saturn, working through the balance and fairness of the Libran scales.

What Justice is telling you

Justice encourages you to be firm and decisive. She advises you to think through your problem carefully, but not to sit on the fence in the hope that it will resolve itself or simply go away. She tells you that whatever path you decide to take, the future is in your hands. An option that seems a difficult and uphill path is likely to turn out well for you in the long term. Do not be afraid of obstacles that appear to be in your way. You have the inner strength to overcome them. Be practical and self-critical, kind, patient, and sympathetic to others who are weaker than yourself.

Questions to ask yourself

Am I being selfish and inconsiderate of others? Am I burying my head in the sand over a problem that is confronting me? Am I thinking just about today and not what will happen to me or others a year or two from now? Do I complain childishly that life isn't fair? If I opt for the difficult decision will I become a better person?

VIIII THE HERMIT

The Hermit is a wise old man who has gathered a wealth of experience and self-knowledge, and now lives a life of reflection and seclusion. He represents turning away from the external world to focus on inner wisdom. In spite of his reclusiveness, he carries a lantern to light the path ahead. This may be symbolic of his quest for knowledge. Sometimes he is accompanied by a serpent, which represents the cycle of death and rebirth. In astrology, the Hermit is related to Jupiter.

What the Hermit is telling you

The Hermit encourages you to increase your knowledge of the world through study and experience. He warns you that you must not rest on your laurels, thinking that you know everything there is to know – whether about subjects that are important to you, or more generally concerning humanity and the universe at large. He suggests that sometimes you need to withdraw and consider your opinions, and be unafraid of making changes to your outlook. He encourages you to keep an open mind and always to be receptive, if sceptical, of new developments. He also warns against stubbornness and suggests that you should seek guidance from others.

Questions to ask yourself

Am I in a rut? Do I need mental stimulation? Should I take up an intellectual challenge? Am I becoming fixed in my opinions and outlook? Has the time come to move on and make changes? Where do I see myself in the future?

KEY WORDS
Truth, knowledge, guidance.

X THE WHEEL OF FORTUNE

The Wheel is kept in balance by a figure who sits at its top and aims to keep the equilibrium. Two creatures are pictured trying to unbalance the wheel. They represent both progress and difficulties. Here is uncertainty – the Wheel could turn in either direction. Sometimes on this card we also find the Angel, Lion, Ox, and Eagle, which represent the Evangelists – the writers of the New Testament's Four Gospels. They offer hope of stability in a constantly changing world. The astrological counterpart of the Wheel is the planet Uranus.

What the Wheel is telling you

Do not be afraid of the unexpected, for it will open new perspectives for you. However, you should try to be sure of your ground and be certain that you have enough experience and knowledge before accepting changes and new conditions, especially if they take you into a different realm from that to which you are accustomed. The Wheel of Fortune suggests that your circumstances seem to be about to change. There is a strong likelihood that you are coming out of a tense or trying period of your life and are now at the beginning of a fresh, new cycle.

Questions to ask yourself

Am I ready for any changes that may occur in my life? Do I need to develop more flexibility in my outlook? Have I been keeping to my safe lifestyle for too long? Is this making me old-fashioned in my outlook? Do I need to move with the times?

KEY WORDS
Equilibrium, change, motion.

XI STRENGTH

KEY WORDS
Fortitude, willpower, triumph.

This strong woman is holding open the jaws of a lion. She represents triumph over difficulties and weakness of character by steady persistence. The lion represents power and positive energy, and she harnesses that power. She achieves her desires by strength of character, fairness, and well-considered intuition. By tradition she wears a hat similar to that of the Magician (*see page 11*), and in some respects her influence is related to his. Strength is sympathetic to the astrological influence of Neptune.

What Strength is telling you

Strength suggests that you should become more aware of your intuition and listen to it. The figure says that you have great emotional power, which, provided it is controlled, will work well for you. Beware of the negative emotion of jealousy. Remember that while anger can be a positive release of feeling, sudden outbursts over minor upsets are unlikely to help matters and may be detrimental not only to others but to yourself. Force also suggests that you should give some thought to your imagination. Consider whether it is causing you to worry unnecessarily, especially about loved ones. Use it positively by being creative.

Questions to ask yourself

Do I always tend to assume that the worst has happened? Do I blame others for my own mistakes? Am I jealous of my partner? Can I be more patient with other people – especially my children? Do I need to relax more? Would I benefit from new creative interests?

XII THE HANGED MAN

Do not be disconcerted by the appearance of the Hanged Man. His expression shows he is neither dead nor even in distress. Sometimes the Hanged Man is pictured holding money bags. These represent riches gathered through experience, resulting from the good influence of others. At present he is in limbo waiting for something to happen. Sometimes he is thought of as a sad, martyred figure; but he is also a symbol of hope. Astrologically, he is related to the zodiac sign Pisces.

What the Hanged Man is telling you

It seems as if you are between two phases in your life, waiting for news before you can move forward. The Hanged Man encourages you not to take premature action. Waiting, not knowing what your next move should be, is difficult, but you must control restlessness and be patient and philosophical in outlook. Accept the fact that you have already achieved a great deal, and trust that your experience will stand you in good stead for what is to come. Be forgiving of those who have harmed you, and aim to balance materialistic progress with spiritual development.

Questions to ask yourself

What is the best way to spend my time during this period of waiting? What preparation can I make for the future, considering the paths that are open to me? Am I avoiding making a decision because I am not facing up to reality? Am I only pretending not to care about the future when my inaction is really caused by cowardliness or laziness?

KEY WORDS
Transformation, progression.

XIII DEATH

This card does not literally mean a death; instead it represents significant change. Death usually wears an unthreatening grin. He is busy with his scythe clearing a path for you on which he encourages you to walk toward the future, uncluttered by past mistakes. Two human heads are also depicted on the card. One usually wears a crown. The other is a lesser mortal. They emphasize that we all, in whatever area of life, experience periods of change that lead to new beginnings.

What Death is telling you

Death says that you are at a crossroads in your life. The time is right for you to cast aside that which you know is finished and make a fresh start. Put past longings and regrets behind you. Don't look back, look forward. Don't keep thinking "if only...". Be brave and open-minded. Be hopeful and positive in outlook. The time is now right to develop new enterprises, projects, and skills. The change in your life can either be self-motivated or it may be thrust upon you. In whatever way change arises, the outcome will be successful and rewarding. Remember that time flies – make good use of it.

Questions to ask yourself

Am I clinging to the past? Am I carefully planning my next move? How financially secure can I make myself? With this in view, should I work harder? Am I, like the ostrich, burying my head in the sand? Am I pretending to be unconcerned about the future when in reality I am fearful of taking action?

KEY WORDS
Change, new beginnings.

XIIII TEMPERANCE

KEY WORDS
Moderation, stability, diligence.

A kindly, beautiful woman carefully pours water from one urn into another. The water represents the essence of life, and the symbol relates to the past merging with the future. Temperance is kind, thoughtful, caring, motherly, and comforting. Flowers are sometimes depicted growing around her feet. She is related to the astrological influence of the Moon in the sign of Taurus.

What Temperance is telling you

Temperance is bringing you a message of encouragement. She says you should take a practical outlook, controlling your emotions but not suppressing them. You should make certain that you enjoy and believe in what you are doing; this will lead to a life of peace and harmony. She adds that you should draw on your natural talents and, if necessary, study a subject that is dear to you. You will then make progress. Temperance warns that short cuts to success do not usually pay off. The slow, steady way leads to a fulfilled life. Always be practical, and while you should, of course, partake of earthly delights and pleasures, you must guard against overindulgence where food and sex are concerned.

Questions to ask yourself

Do I have any long-standing, unfulfilled desires? Do I react possessively toward my loved ones? Is our sex life rewarding to my partner as well as myself? Am I lethargic? Do I need more exercise, or to regulate my eating/drinking habits? Am I practical with money, or do I tend to be extravagant?

XV THE DEVIL

Our Devil is seen in traditional form, putting fear into our hearts – but for our own good. He shows us the error of our ways and highlights the failings of ignorance. Humanity is represented by the two figures he has tied to the plinth. He has power over them, but in his wisdom he has made their shackles loose enough for them to escape. It is they who are foolish if they do not take advantage of this, and release themselves from their situation. The Devil is related to the zodiac sign Scorpio.

What the Devil is telling you

You must become aware that you, and only you, can rid yourself of the psychological bonds that inhibit you. Self-analysis is a useful tool to help you sort out your personal problems. The Devil also says that having given your concerns considerable thought, you should not spend fruitless hours dwelling on them. To avoid brooding on problems requires considerable conscious effort, but will help you attain psychological wholeness. Concentrating on positive aspects in your personality should help you to overcome weaknesses and will make you happier. The Devil insists that you are not as trapped in your problems or situation as you may think.

Questions to ask yourself

Am I brooding over the past? Am I obsessive about my difficulties? Can I look at them from another perspective? Should I seek professional help? Am I smoking, taking drugs, or drinking too much? If so, why? Am I ignoring my problems or avoiding the truth?

KEY WORDS
Self-awareness, revelation.

XVI THE TOWER

A solidly built tower has been struck by a bolt of lightning causing shock and disaster to its inhabitants. The destruction of the Tower symbolizes the sudden end of a job or a relationship and the possibility of new and better opportunities. A crown is often depicted falling from the top of the Tower, representing the destruction of vanity and conceit. The tower's small windows suggest a self-protective element is present that can lead to a limited outlook on life. The Tower is related to the astrological influence of Mars.

What the Tower is telling you

The Tower is warning you that you are in danger of taking serious risks. It is telling you to be more cautious and careful in all your dealings – financial, personal, and physical.

You are also accident-prone at present, so consciously slow down– especially while driving, or handling dangerous tools, knives, or hot dishes. The Tower indicates important and unexpected change, perhaps a complete break from what you have built up over a long period of time. If you are cautious in all areas of your life, the Tower says that you will benefit from any clean sweep you make – providing you keep that element of blind risk-taking firmly under control.

Questions to ask yourself

Am I being rash in my attitude to life? Am I being arrogant about my achievements? Is my proposed line of action self-centered? Will I or my family suffer if I take this step? Have I seriously considered what is ahead?

KEY WORDS
Risks, downfall, drastic change.

XVII THE STAR

KEY WORDS
Hope, inspiration, idealism.

The young woman depicted on this card is Persephone of Greek legend, who spent one-third of every year with Hades, the god of the underworld, and two-thirds with her mother, the earth goddess Demeter. Persephone is pouring water to fertilize and nurture the land. The large star is the one seen by the Magi, while the smaller stars represent hope. The vigorous shrubs and plants symbolize renewal and rebirth. The Star is related to the astrological influence of the Moon in Pisces.

What the Star is telling you

The Star suggests that you should be positive in outlook, and that while you may look to the stars for guidance you should also make a practical effort to achieve your heart's desire. Avoid daydreaming and nurturing

unattainable fantasies. Keep your feet firmly on the ground and by practical effort you will grow, psychologically and spiritually. Beware of untruthfulness or deceptiveness. Someone in your life is a powerful guiding light – take notice of what he or she says. The Star is a brilliant and positive influence. Take her advice and you will gain in self-confidence and travel far along life's interesting path.

Questions to ask yourself

Are my objectives realistic or unattainable? Is my outlook as practical as it should be? Do I tend to daydream and waste precious time? Am I using my imagination and creative talent in a positive, practical way? Am I being self-deceptive or untruthful? If so, is this taking the easy way out of tricky situations?

XVIII THE MOON

The Moon dominates the images on this card. She is beautiful, but the light she sheds on the world is deceptive; under it we tend not to see things as they really are. Wolflike dogs are baying at her – they do not trust her influence. A deep pool of water is home to a crablike creature. This represents our innermost feelings and emotions, which, if we keep hidden as the creature hides within its hard shell, causes us to be unhappy and unfulfilled. The Moon is related to the zodiac sign Cancer.

What the Moon is telling you

The Moon suggests that you should allow yourself a greater freedom of expression and avoid holding back or suppressing your feelings. Contrarily, it can also suggest that you have reacted overemotionally to a certain

situation in your life. The Moon hints that you may be allowing your emotions to affect your judgment. You may be living under some kind of illusion and refusing to see things as they really are. In the long run, self-deception will harm you and you must face up to reality. The Moon warns you to be wary of consulting friends: they could be much less trustworthy than you imagine.

Questions to ask yourself

Am I being illogical at present? Have I looked at my problems from a purely practical point of view? Has someone too much influence over my judgment? Is my imagination running away with me? Am I holding back when I should let my feelings be known? Am I over-reacting to a situation?

KEY WORDS
Emotion, intuition, illusion.

XVIIII THE SUN

The Sun casts strong rays of light on a loving couple who represent love, friendship, and rapport. They are protected from outside evil influences by a sturdy, well-built, but quite low wall. However, we get the impression that the couple are becoming overheated by the Sun's powerful influence. They are beginning to perspire and will have to take action to prevent discomfort. The Sun is related to the zodiac sign Leo.

What the Sun is telling you

A symbol of fulfillment and joy, the Sun suggests you should burn up your creative powers and energy in a positive way through work and rewarding interests. You should make sure your leisure activities are enjoyable and satisfying. You will receive pleasure from the arts. The Sun advises exercise and activity to avoid lethargy, which leads to missed opportunities and wasting precious time. However, you must beware of over-exertion, which can lead to physical and emotional burnout. The Sun tells you that you have excellent organizational skills that you should use to encourage others to enjoy life. If you are thinking about starting or increasing your family, the Sun gives you his blessing.

Questions to ask yourself

Do I try to get enjoyment and fulfillment out of every day? Do I enjoy my work? Do I need to fill my leisure hours in a more enjoyable way? Am I wasting my latent creativity? Am I bossy toward other people or do I encourage them to have fun? Am I lethargic?

KEY WORDS
Vitality, energy, self-expression.

XX THE JUDGMENT

KEY WORDS
Transformation, progress.

Here is an angel blowing his trumpet to waken the dead from their graves and tell them it is Judgment Day. The dead are praying for mercy in the hope that the sins of their lifetimes will be forgiven. They now know that their misdemeanors are being exposed, and they are hoping to be allowed to move onto a higher plane of existence. The Judgment is related to the astrological influence of Pluto.

What the Judgment is telling you

The Judgment is saying that at this point in your life it is time to assess yourself and evaluate your achievements. You should address any psychological problems which, up to now, you have ignored. You should try to analyze any problems so that in future your progress is not hindered by unnecessary hang-ups. The Judgment tells you to judge yourself because you need to be far more self-aware. To keep your psyche in balance you must also give yourself credit for positive personality traits because they will help you to overcome that which is negative. The Judgment emphasizes that you should be fair to yourself. If you can do this you will, like the symbolic people of the card, move on to live life on a higher and more worthwhile level of existence.

Questions to ask yourself

Is there room for improvement in the way I treat other people? Do I have a tendency to be selfish and self-centered? Should I be more sympathetic and less resentful? Am I unnecessarily inhibited and shy? Do I allow my inner voice to put me down?

XXI THE WORLD

The World is represented by a woman surrounded by a laurel wreath. It is obvious that she has succeeded in all her ventures. She is supported by the symbols of the Evangelists – Angel, Lion, Ox, and Eagle. They, the guardians of truth, have supported her along her chosen path, and now she can "rest on her laurels," having achieved all she has set out to do. Astrologically, the World seems to be most strongly related to the Midheaven, which is the highest point in the sky at the moment of birth.

What the World is telling you

The World is congratulating you. She symbolizes completion, self-knowledge, and success. She suggests that you remind yourself of what you have already achieved, and know that others are aware of you and appreciate your past efforts. She tells you that you are now entering an extremely rewarding phase of your life, when you will enjoy the benefits of all your hard work. Here is ultimate happiness and inner satisfaction. Enjoying your time to the fullest in any way that you know will bring you further pleasure and sheer joy. This is a superb card.

Questions to ask yourself

First of all, give yourself a hearty pat on the back – you deserve it, and we think that you probably do not have any questions to ask yourself! Nevertheless you might consider, having achieved so much, how you can best use your experience further to develop your own intellect and the intellects of others.

KEY WORDS
Achievement, inner satisfaction.

THE MINOR ARCANA

The Minor Arcana consists of 56 cards that are divided into four suits: Cups, Wands, Pentacles, and Swords. Each correlate to the Hearts, Clubs, Diamonds, and Spades of conventional playing cards. Each suit is ruled by its royal family, known as the Court cards, which has four members unlike the three of ordinary packs of playing cards. The additional family member is the Knight.

QUEEN OF WANDS

PAGE OF CUPS

THE FOUR SUITS

Each of the suits consists of four Court cards and ten numbered cards. The Cups represent our emotions, the way in which we express our love for others, and our all-important needs in this area. These cards relate to the passionate side of love, and the pleasure we obtain from sex. They are also related to our unconscious, our intuition, our imagination – and to the way in which we express anger.

The Wands, also known as Batons or Clubs, represent action and our sense of and need for adventure. We are praised for what we have achieved and can achieve, and warned when we must expect demanding challenges. Wands often reveal the true reason why we are uncertain about our next move, and warn of when we may face stress. They also suggest when to keep calm and relax, and when to be energetic and bold.

The Pentacles, also known as Discs or Coins, comment on the way we make and spend money, on how hard we work, and on our practical problems. They advise us how to develop financial ability and warn us against extravagance. They caution us against becoming too acquisitive, careless, or indiscreet, and focus too on the practical side of our chosen career or profession.

The Swords represent mental activity and agility – how we cope with problems and make decisions. They suggest when we should study or accept intellectual challenge. They show us how to cope with responsibility, and warn us when such burdens are likely to increase. Symbolically, they are concerned with opposition, delay, and difficulty – yet almost always find some way of helping and encouraging us.

THE COURT CARDS

The Court cards usually represent significant people in the querent's life, such as parents, teachers, or employers. Occasionally they represent the concepts for which they stand, such as ambition or caring. The King and Queen often represent someone who is clearly part of the situation under consideration. The Knight is a messenger bringing a missive to the querent. He also focuses on our thoughts, or encourages us to think about our problems in a different way. It is worth considering whether he may be related to some other Court card which will, in turn, represent someone in your life. The Pages, known as the Knaves in some packs, represent young people, from babies to people in their early twenties. These younger people can be male or female and are often a member of the querent's family.

It is important to consider the placing of a Court card in your spread. For instance, you may well find the King of Pentacles in the "distant past." In that position he represents someone in your past who fits his description, who might now be dead, or who now has less influence on you than previously. When a male card is reversed it represents a woman; when a female card is reversed it represents a man.

THE PIP CARDS

The numbered cards of the suits are known as the Pip cards. While they are closely related to their suit and what it represents, they also show our own position within the situation under consideration. To help you understand the Pips, key words of each of the respective card numbers are shown in the box below. The Pip cards support the advice and messages from the cards of the Major Arcana. The individual meanings of the cards are related to the collective meaning of the suit to which they belong. The same number within each suit – such as the Five of Cups, Wands, Pentacles, and Swords – represents the same principle. But each suit relates to a different sphere of life, so the numbered card of one suit sometimes has the opposite meaning to the same numbered card of another suit. For example, success is the basic principal of the sevens. However, while the Seven of Cups indicates success for yourself and loved ones, the Seven of Swords represents the success of rivals or opponents.

Bear in mind that while the Pip cards often relate to the future, if one appears in the "distant past" section of a spread, it represents your situation as it was then. When it appears in a section of a spread relating to the future, it suggests how you will (not necessarily should!) relate to the future development of the situation that is being considered – emotionally, for instance, if it is the Ace of Cups, or with confidence in your financial security if it is the Ace of Pentacles. There might be problems with communications if the Ace of Swords appears, while the Ace of Wands would suggest that you will be particularly self-disciplined. As you use the cards, you will gradually learn how each of the cards with the same number can represent the same theme or stage of development, while their individual meaning, according to their suit, is very different.

Remember to look at cards in relation to the others that come before and after them in a spread. Cards do not stand alone. With practice, you will learn to read a spread as a whole, rather than as individual cards.

KEY WORDS OF THE MINOR ARCANA

CUPS	*emotion, the unconscious, fantasy, intuition*
WANDS	*action, adventure, achievement, challenge*
PENTACLES	*prosperity, hard work, financial progress, practical concerns*
SWORDS	*mental activity, truth, tact, fairness*

ACES	*commencement*	SIXES	*opposition may succeed*
TWOS	*opposition*	SEVENS	*success*
THREES	*realization*	EIGHTS	*partial success*
FOURS	*obstacles*	NINES	*equilibrium*
FIVES	*victory*	TENS	*conclusion*

CUPS

Cups are the equivalent of Hearts in ordinary playing cards. This family is perhaps the most understanding of the four suits. They symbolize pleasure, love, the unconscious, and intuition. This is a happy family whose members are passionate and have deep feelings.

KING OF CUPS

KING OF CUPS

The elderly King is relaxed and authoritative, and is wearing an alert, philosophical expression. He is in a very secure position. He is well-educated and perhaps a bachelor – one who is interested in business and the law. He has read extensively and learned from experience. He is at peace with his emotions, since he is turning away from the Cup that symbolizes them. He is artistic and creative, and might be very good at languages. His negative qualities can make him crafty, dishonest, and capable of double-dealing. We shouldn't believe everything he says, and should beware of his immense charm.

QUEEN OF CUPS

The Queen appears to be a well-balanced person, as she sits on her throne holding her beautiful Cup and the scepter that symbolizes the power with which she reigns. She is very honest and loving, intelligent, intuitive, and practical. Her artistic leaning is toward poetry, and she uses her imagination in a controlled and positive way. She may have musical talent, or at least be very appreciative of music. Her negative qualities could make her prone to unnecessary worry, and she has a tendency to dramatize minor problems. This can give her a poor sense of perspective. She probably needs to develop a more rational outlook on life, although it may not be easy to give her such sound advice.

QUEEN OF CUPS

KNIGHT OF CUPS

The Knight is a messenger bringing you an invitation or news of some important opportunity to which you should give serious thought. But he is somewhat romantic and dreamy, and can be untrustworthy. Whatever is going on in his mind, it seems that he is anxious for you to receive his message because he is already holding out to you the Cup that contains it, rather than clutching it to his own chest. You should be quite clear in your own mind what the message is, and what is to be expected of you. In other words be cautious and somewhat skeptical of any proposition put to you. Try to further develop your powers of concentration.

PAGE OF CUPS

Here is an obedient young person who is gazing into his Cup; we assume that he is considering his emotional life and his loves. He is calm and able to be objective in any situation. We might say that this youngster is old for his years. He takes his educational studies very seriously and will eventually do extremely well. We have confidence in him, and know that he is maturing fast – already learning from experience. At times he may be somewhat withdrawn and shy, so he should try to develop more extroverted tendencies. He seems not to be a particularly energetic person and may not be interested in sports and exercise, so perhaps needs encouragement to take part in more physical activity.

ACE OF CUPS

This card indicates a love affair, or news of someone dear to you. There is a possibility of advantageous travel for family reasons. Advice from a friend will prove worthwhile.

TWO OF CUPS

Be cautious with your emotions: otherwise you could commit yourself to a new lover who will prove unworthy. If already in a relationship, know that your love is reciprocated. Rather differently, an involvement with someone who shares your intellectual interests will be beneficial.

THREE OF CUPS

A difficult problem will soon be resolved. Romance could well be in the air; and if you are about to be married, know that your union is blessed with true love and happiness. Creative work makes excellent progress. This card warns that you might be overindulgent and hypersensitive.

FOUR OF CUPS

There is a possibility of an increase in your family, and signs of long-lasting love and affection. However, you must be prepared for certain obstacles hindering your progress. Do not yield to inner discontent. Be intuitive when encountering difficulties and you will get through.

FIVE OF CUPS

You must beware of reacting over-sensitively to any remark or situation. If you control the flow of your emotion you will achieve your desire, but any tendency toward the dramatic will hinder your progress.

SIX OF CUPS

You will be dynamically attracted to another person, which will prove exciting; but do not make hasty decisions while in this mood. This card suggests a happy event within your family or circle of friends.

SEVEN OF CUPS

Here is success for yourself and your loved ones. If planning to move to a new home, you will be happy there. Any misunderstanding that has bothered you recently will soon become a thing of the past.

EIGHT OF CUPS

You are likely to encounter difficulties in your relationship. Consider whether you are being selfish. You may need to develop joint interests or improve communication. Make an effort to discuss your problems calmly.

NINE OF CUPS

Here is indication of emotional stability and joy in your role as a parent. A change in your domestic life will prove to be beneficial. This card also warns that you may be prone to jealousy. You could be reacting negatively to some incident for no good reason.

TEN OF CUPS

Here is an indication of a happy family life, success, and fulfillment. If you are looking for a new home, there is a good chance that you will find one. Long-distance travel is a distinct possibility – enjoy!

WANDS

Wands, the equivalent of Clubs in playing cards, symbolize energy and growth. The royal Wands are inventive and always eager to see projects through to a satisfactory conclusion. They are hardworking, and their enthusiasm is extremely infectious.

KNIGHT OF WANDS

PAGE OF WANDS

KING OF WANDS

Here is a young, enthusiastic king, perhaps given to restlessness and with little time to spare. He is confident and very modern in his ways. Notice how informally he sits on his throne, and his alert expression. He is noble and honest but his emotions are easily inflamed, which makes him short-tempered at times. Nevertheless, he is capable of achieving a great deal. He is a good father figure, and a very lively person. His main faults – of which he may well not be fully aware, no matter how many times they are pointed out to him – are that he can be pompous and dogmatic. He needs to cultivate flexibility of mind and outlook.

QUEEN OF WANDS

The Queen is young and beautiful, and appears to be thoroughly at one with herself and at ease in her important position. She is usually very honest and has a great deal of common sense. She is open-minded, and not as dogmatic or fixed in her opinions as her husband. She feels great sympathy for others less fortunate than herself, and will comfort them when they are in trouble. She is also extremely feminine and will always be fashionable and wear expensive and beautiful clothes. However, she has her faults, and at times she can become very jealous. She also has the propensity to be deceitful.

KNIGHT OF WANDS

This Knight is totally fearless. He is ready to accept everything that the future holds for him. When he features in your cards, he encourages you to think positively and optimistically about the future, and to face it unflinchingly. The way he holds his Wand shows that he is handing on to you all his positive, assertive qualities, which you must express to the fullest. His message is that you would greatly profit from the experience of adventurous travel. He warns that you may encounter difficulties with your partner, and perhaps you will have a change in your relationships. He also suggests that you should think about new ways to expand your career and business interests.

PAGE OF WANDS

This family's Page is untroubled by personal problems; he seems to be at peace with the world as he philosophically contemplates his Wand, which is firmly planted on the ground. It represents future developments, which he looks forward to with confidence. He is trustworthy and loyal. He will be a good friend who will let no one down, and we know that what we tell him will be treated in the greatest confidence. His advice will be sound and he is very reliable. He is warning you against indecision, and of problems which might be generated by unkind gossip. You are fortunate indeed to have a person like this youngster within your family or circle of friends.

ACE OF WANDS

News of a new business opportunity is coming your way. Challenge seems likely, so to achieve what you wish you may have to be aggressive; but control any tendency to ruthlessness. An important phone call, fax, or email could make a considerable difference to your future.

TWO OF WANDS

You will overcome any present obstacles through persistence of effort. There is indication of success through considerable expenditure of time and energy in career or business interests. There is a possibility of promotion, or simply a nice surprise awaiting you.

THREE OF WANDS

Your business partnerships will prove to be successful. You can afford to be self-confident and even aggressive in your dealings, since lively action will get excellent results. Your enthusiasm is infectious; it will not be difficult for you to win other people over to your way of thinking.

FOUR OF WANDS

You will overcome present difficulties, which leads to more successful enterprises and to praise from associates. There is a possibility of promotion and prosperity. An inheritance may be coming to you.

FIVE OF WANDS

You will have to cope with fierce competition, but your determination will pay off. On no account ignore the advice that more experienced people give you – it will be very sensible and, even if critical, constructive.

SIX OF WANDS

Be prepared for failure when success seems within your grasp. It will help if you take a philosophical attitude to any delays you encounter. Patience will increase the possibility of eventual success. Extremes of action or speech in business or career matters should be avoided at all costs.

SEVEN OF WANDS

Your enterprise will be rewarded. Calculated risks will pay off. The present strength of your position shows that rivals don't stand a chance of overtaking you. You are now in a progressive and rewarding period.

EIGHT OF WANDS

You must think before taking the initiative – any impulsive actions will cause setbacks. Keep calm and try not to force any issue, since that will show impulsiveness. Caution will lead to the promotion you desire.

NINE OF WANDS

New developments in your career will turn out to be favorable for you. If you encounter difficulties you can rely on your intuition and prudence to see you through. Your knowledge of human nature is a great asset.

TEN OF WANDS

You are about to achieve something that is very important to you, but this is not the time to ignore help from colleagues. Instead, encourage team spirit and your colleagues will admire your reasonable attitude.

PENTACLES

Pentacles, the equivalent of Diamonds in ordinary playing cards, represent the materialistic world of finance and worldly progress; but they also comment on the relationship between you and your work, and how important your involvement in it is.

QUEEN OF PENTACLES

PAGE OF PENTACLES

KING OF PENTACLES

This King is a successful man who has a sharp business sense. He is shrewd and clever, and misses no opportunities. Notice that his hat is shaped like a figure eight. This shows that he is sympathetic to the symbolism of The Magician (Major Arcana I), and Strength (Major Arcana XI). Here we have some Mercurial influences at work. This King can be here, there, and everywhere to further his business projects. He loves the material comfort that his hard work brings about, and he is a very loyal friend. He is, however, very prone to restlessness, a little too fond of gambling, and sometimes has a reckless tendency to speculate.

QUEEN OF PENTACLES

The Queen of Pentacles is a very satisfied creature – we might even say self-satisfied – as she gazes at her treasure. She is a trifle smug, too, but kind and motherly, generous and charitable to those less well-off than herself. However, she does like all her kindnesses and gifts to be thoroughly appreciated. Financial security is all-important to her, yet she will spend a great deal on her clothes and her home, as she, like her husband, enjoys her creature comforts. She uses her energy to make her home luxurious, and likes to gives the impression of expensive good taste. Although she is secure, she is very fearful of failure and more cautious than her husband, for whom she shows considerable concern from time to time. She tends to be not entirely trustful of other people.

KNIGHT OF PENTACLES

This Knight is a fine fellow who overcomes obstacles and has no difficulty in attaining his goals. He is mature and reliable, and is asking you whether you are thinking about investments for the future. He suggests that you should take sound financial advice and plan for your retirement. In a really positive mood, he may be bringing news of an unexpected financial gain. He also has a bearing on health, and asks whether you are feeling well. If not, he suggests that you may need some additional vitamins, or perhaps have a checkup with your doctor.

PAGE OF PENTACLES

Although looking at his Pentacle, this Page seems to be rather bored by it – or at best simply deciding what to buy next. He probably allows cash to slip through his fingers – the way he is holding the Pentacle, it looks as if he is going to hurl it into the distance like a discus thrower. He seems superficially free of care. He is a dreamer and has poor powers of concentration. Nevertheless, he has plenty of originality and is brighter than first impressions might suggest. In fact, once he has come to decisions about his future he could easily become totally absorbed by what it has to offer and make excellent progress. It is at this stage in his life that his natural determination and willpower will begin to blossom.

ACE OF PENTACLES

A turn of fortune. If you are waiting for some payment, it will come. While you enjoy entertaining, be warned that your generosity will prove to be more expensive than you had planned. You are not lacking in bright ideas at present, and your versatility will stand you in good stead.

TWO OF PENTACLES

Your ingenuity will bring about unexpected financial gain, so persist with any enterprise that calls upon your skill, originality, and mental effort. You may gain financially through social activities.

THREE OF PENTACLES

In your enthusiasm for what is happening in your life you may be indiscreet. Be cautious – a word to the wrong person might spoil your plans or hard work. Travel for business will be positive.

FOUR OF PENTACLES

You are vulnerable to financial difficulties. You must reconsider or re-organize your financial arrangements in order to improve your bank balance. Do not hoard what you know to be worn out or mere clutter.

FIVE OF PENTACLES

Any losses you may have incurred will be retrieved, and discussions with a partner will lead to an easing of financial difficulties. At this point in your life you could benefit, financially and intellectually, from a course of study. Some legal documents may be on their way to you.

SIX OF PENTACLES

You will do well to share your profits with others. Perhaps you should be generous to family members, or make a donation to a favorite charity. You may be feeling somewhat depressed at the moment. If so, spend time with, and talk to, a friend who you know will lift your spirits.

SEVEN OF PENTACLES

The fruits of your hard work will be reaped and you are assured of financial success. General financial progress is assured, as is the possibility of a very successful business trip. Your future looks secure.

EIGHT OF PENTACLES

Although you will gain success, you could feel inner dissatisfaction. Perhaps you are less fulfilled than you would like: you may need intellectual stimulation, or simply be in need of more exercise.

NINE OF PENTACLES

Financial security is indicated. You may receive an unexpected gift that is outweighed by an equally unexpected bill. You are probably working hard and are vulnerable to a buildup of stress. Make certain you put time aside for restorative relaxation.

TEN OF PENTACLES

Any business deals in which you are involved will go through smoothly. While you can afford to be inventive when investing, you should be cautious: because you are on a winning streak you could easily overinvest.

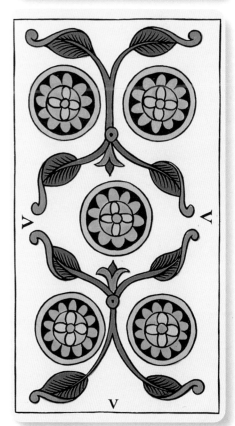

SWORDS

Swords, the equivalent of Spades in ordinary playing cards, represent mental strength, courage, authority, achievement, and ambition. They encourage activity and applaud accomplishment. The presence of a Sword card in a spread is often indicative of change.

KING OF SWORDS

KING OF SWORDS

The King is inquisitive and ambitious, and has an intelligent and alert expression. He is sympathetic to the Chariot (Major Arcana VII). He is a very powerful personality and his word is law. His unsheathed Sword indicates that he is ready for action at any time. He is determined and has an analytical mind. He would do well as a doctor, engineer, or member of the armed forces, and has excellent powers of leadership. He encourages others to be cautious, but he can be cruel and selfish at times.

QUEEN OF SWORDS

The Queen wears a somewhat troubled expression. She frowns easily, and we realize that she has suffered a lot over the years. She has learned from bitter experience, but this has left its mark on her. She finds it difficult to put tragic happenings behind her and constantly dwells on them. She could represent a widow, or someone coming to terms with bereavement. She is generous and kind, but tends to worry a great deal, and can be narrowminded with a tendency to nag. She is very quick-witted and asks a great many questions, since she is very inquisitive. It is up to us to remind her of the happy events she has experienced, and to encourage her to become involved in new, intellectually demanding interests, for she tends to stagnate.

KNIGHT OF SWORDS

Here is a lively fellow, keen on combat and happy to face adversity. He is very brave and always ready for action. He will confront every problem and difficulty head-on. He will rush fearlessly into the unknown without a single care, or consideration of any good advice he has been given – he all too often gives way to hastiness and impulsiveness. Rather differently, this Knight can also represent someone who is single-minded to the exclusion of all ideas, concepts, or ways of life outside his present situation. His presence is indicative of someone who is overconfident, and his personality traits are a warning that perhaps you are jumping in where angels fear to tread! His message urges caution, and is a warning against taking premature action.

KNIGHT OF SWORDS

PAGE OF SWORDS

This young man is extremely ambitious, alert to every new opportunity that comes his way. He is always vigilant and active. He will enjoy sports and all forms of physical exercise. However, we notice that he holds his unsheathed sword in his left hand, so tradition decrees that his ambitious and energetic qualities may not be obvious. His powers of insight are excellent, but he is not totally trustworthy and cannot entirely be relied upon. The Page also has a bearing on health. He tells you not to continue to ignore any nagging symptom, and to go to your doctor for a checkup. Like all the Sword royal family, he has a sense of humor.

ACE OF SWORDS

You may encounter communication problems. Expect delays in response to any project or idea you have put to superiors. Be flexible, not stubborn. Accept that you may well have to work hard for less than you expect.

TWO OF SWORDS

Here are several warnings. You may have problems as the result of a friend or associate's actions. You are at risk of making sacrifices for other people, who will not appreciate them. Be careful – someone is not being as straight or as honest toward you as they should be.

THREE OF SWORDS

Be prepared for a certain amount of delay and difficulty. There is a possibility of some misunderstanding or deception. Keep an open mind and be ready to collaborate with others should they suggest it. Proceed with caution in all your activities.

FOUR OF SWORDS

The card is a warning that you might easily offend a friend, and you must guard against negative emotions such as jealousy or envy. Be brave and resolute and you will overcome all your difficulties.

FIVE OF SWORDS

Be discreet and cautious, and know that while the path ahead is not easy, with insight and alertness you will win. If involved in any legal battle, the case will eventually be settled in your favor. You need to work hard, but you will see that your efforts have proven really worthwhile.

SIX OF SWORDS

You are in a fortunate position because your rivals are powerless, but you will do well to be disciplined, and to make sure that your work is well-organized. Have a strong sense of purpose and delegate work to others.

SEVEN OF SWORDS

You are at risk of dishonesty. Do not be resentful or jealous of others' success; it will do you no good. Be philosophical; in due course you will come up with a brilliant idea or plan that will put you firmly ahead.

EIGHT OF SWORDS

Allow any important issue to "stew" until difficulties have passed. Follow your instincts: you will know when the time is right to make a move. You need to think clearly, so don't allow others' opinions to confuse you.

NINE OF SWORDS

You need to be careful about your words and actions. Admitting you are wrong will resolve the problem. Uncharacteristic worry may be dogging your progress, so aim to look at any complication in an objective light.

TEN OF SWORDS

You have had financial setbacks or have lost your job. The situation is temporary, and you will soon see a light on the horizon. Do not take any unconventional actions that you think might improve your situation – they won't! Weather any storm you encounter with fortitude and patience.

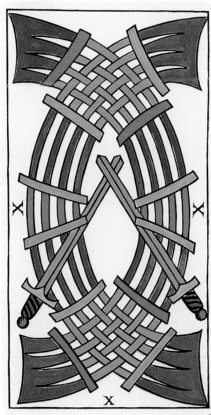

TAROT – A CASE HISTORY

AMY IS STUDYING A SUBJECT THAT IS VERY IMPORTANT TO HER. SHE HAS ALREADY
PASSED HER FIRST EXAMS AND IS NOW WORKING TOWARD HER DEGREE. SHE IS
COMMITTED, BUT HER HUSBAND, ROBERT, FEELS EXCLUDED BY HER STUDIES, AND
THIS IS CAUSING A SERIOUS RIFT BETWEEN THEM. WHAT SHOULD SHE DO?

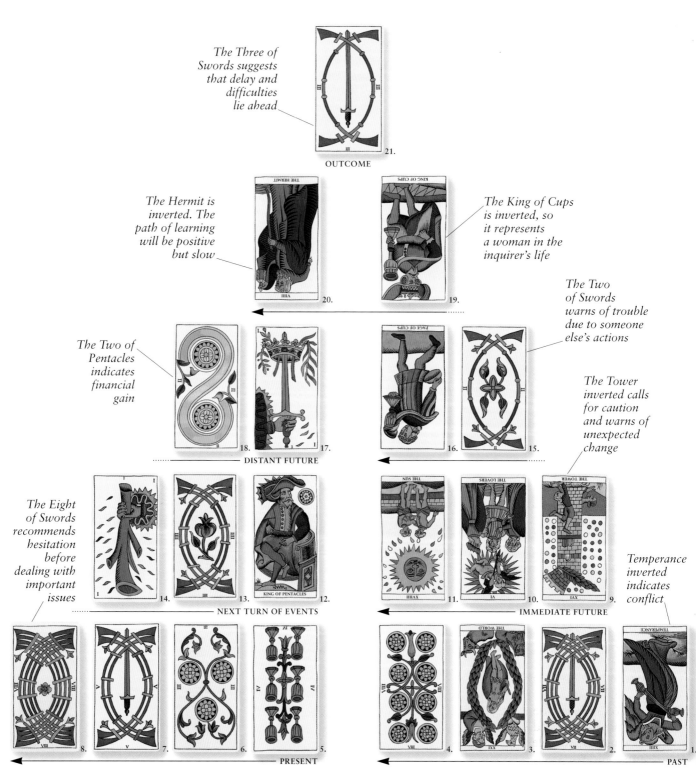

The Three of Swords suggests that delay and difficulties lie ahead

OUTCOME

The Hermit is inverted. The path of learning will be positive but slow

The King of Cups is inverted, so it represents a woman in the inquirer's life

The Two of Swords warns of trouble due to someone else's actions

The Two of Pentacles indicates financial gain

The Tower inverted calls for caution and warns of unexpected change

DISTANT FUTURE

The Eight of Swords recommends hesitation before dealing with important issues

Temperance inverted indicates conflict

NEXT TURN OF EVENTS

IMMEDIATE FUTURE

PRESENT

PAST

OVERALL LOOK AT THE SPREAD

For Amy's question, we used the Pyramid spread because it gives a very detailed view of the situation, and is likely to make useful suggestions. We recommend that you read the interpretation of each card on pages 10–27, and then look at the spread to see which are key cards and how they relate to the passage of time. There are 11 inverted cards, which indicates that Amy's progress and the resolution of her problems will be slow. There is also a predominance of Swords, indicating mental activity and the need for truth, tact, and fairness.

PAST

1. *Temperance, inverted*. Amy has had to take Temperance's message to heart: it sums up the questions she had to ask herself before embarking on her course of study.
2. *Seven of Swords*. She needed to proceed with care and has had to face up to the resentment that she feels is underlying her husband's reactions.
3. *The World, inverted*. This card clearly shows her success in passing the first section. The inversion accentuates delay – Amy had to resubmit one of her papers.
4. *Eight of Pentacles*. She is encouraged to continue her studies. This card relates well to the previous one.

PRESENT

5. *Six of Cups, inverted*. A key card. This card represents an attraction to another person. Amy realizes that this is the close woman friend with whom she often studies.
6. *Three of Pentacles, inverted*. Here is the possibility of a working partnership – again a reference to Amy's fellow student friend. There is a warning – she could have problems to resolve in that relationship.
7. *Five of Swords*. If Amy proceeds with care and works very hard she will be rewarded with success.
8. *Eight of Swords*. She will encounter an uphill struggle in the weeks ahead. The card also suggests that she allow her most important issue (Robert's reactions) to "stew" for the time being.

IMMEDIATE FUTURE

9. *The Tower, inverted*. A key card. Another warning against risk-taking. There is a need for caution and the possibility of important, unexpected changes.
10. *The Lovers, inverted*. The Lovers want her to be happy, and they ask if she is doing everything she can to understand Robert and what he wants to achieve. They warn against senseless bickering and say that compromise and some sacrifices will be worthwhile.

11. *The Sun, inverted*. Here is encouragement for Amy to use her creative powers in a positive way.

NEXT TURN OF EVENTS

12. *King of Pentacles*. This is a very accurate description of Robert.
13. *Four of Swords*. A key card, and very positive. As it follows the King of Pentacles, representing Robert, its message is clear. Amy must be brave; persistence of effort will see her through her difficulties with him.
14. *Ace of Wands, inverted*. She must be disciplined and orderly in her work. Good opportunities are coming her way. This is important to Amy – she knows she needs this message.
15. *Two of Swords*. The card warns of trouble, perhaps due to a friend's or associate's action. Amy is at risk of making too many sacrifices for others. She knows that she is being somewhat held back by her friend, who works at a much slower pace than she does.
16. *Page of Cups, inverted*. The young person is an exact description of Amy and Robert's 16-year-old daughter, who is very objective about her parents.

DISTANT FUTURE

17. *Ace of Swords*. A key card. Amy may experience some problems in receiving communications. She must expect delays, but must keep an open mind. If she feels depressed (about her work and situation) she must realize that these feelings will pass.
18. *Two of Pentacles*. Her ingenuity will bring financial gain. There is a possibility of her forming a business partnership in future.
19. *King of Cups, inverted*. This description represents an older woman who is more experienced in Amy's subject. She helps and encourages Amy. (Remember, as the King is inverted he represents a woman.)
20. *The Hermit, inverted*. This is a particularly interesting card to be so near the top of Amy's spread. Here we have knowledge and wisdom – which Amy will gain as she proceeds with her studies. She must keep an open mind and be on the lookout for new developments and changes in her subject. She must be receptive, but skeptical. We must, however, remember that the Hermit is inverted, like so many of Amy's cards. Her path is a long, slow, uphill one; but it is positive and progressive.

OUTCOME

21. *Three of Swords*. A key card. Here is a tricky card at number 21. It says that Amy must be prepared for delay and difficulties, which supports the general theme of the spread. It expresses the need for caution, and it is a card that often indicates important changes.

RUNES

THE ANCIENT NORSE TRIBES OF EUROPE ARE BELIEVED TO HAVE USED A RUNIC ALPHABET OVER 2,000 YEARS AGO. MAGIC POWERS WERE THOUGHT TO INHABIT THE SYMBOLS THAT WERE SCRATCHED ON ARMOR, JEWELS, AND TOMBSTONES – INDEED THE EARLIEST FORM OF THE WORD "RUNE" MEANT "MYSTERY" OR "SECRET" IN THE OLD NORSE LANGUAGE.

God of Fertility

The first eight runes of the Elder Futhark are known as Frey's Aett, after the Norse god of fertility and summer. This 11th-century Viking bronze depicting Frey comes from Sweden.

THE ORIGINS OF THE RUNES THAT WE KNOW TODAY ARE DISPUTED. URUNNEN MAY HAVE BEEN A PREHISTORIC ALPHABET AND A POSSIBLE forerunner of the Mediterranean and Phoenician alphabets, though there are many other theories. Some scholars believe that the Greek alphabet of the sixth century BC came before the runes, others that the Latin alphabet was its origin; yet again a new theory proposes that runic script developed from a North Etruscan, Alpine alphabet.

What cannot be disputed is that the runes are ancient, and that from early in their history they were associated with magic powers and purposes. As with so many other areas of magic, the growth of the Roman Catholic Church drove the use of runes underground – but there are records of their use right through to the present day. Fifty of the earliest runic symbols were in use in Denmark and Schleswig, Germany, in the third century AD. In Norway, 200 years later, 60 runic symbols were to be found, and 50 more Anglo-Saxon ones date from AD 650–750. In Sweden in the 11th and 12th centuries AD, no less than 2,500 different runic symbols were recorded. These were used both for magic purposes and for writing poems and genealogies.

THE RUNE FAMILIES

In this pack, we use the standard Elder Futhark (Futhark being the name of the Norse alphabet), consisting of 24 runes, to which we have added the more recent innovation of the blank rune, Wyrd (*see page 41*).

Rather like the four elements that relate to the 12 zodiac signs and the four suits of the Tarot, the 24 runes are divided into three "families" of eight members called Aetts, which are named after three gods of the Norse pantheon. The first eight runes are known as Frey's Aett, named after Frey, the Norse god of fertility. The next eight runes are called Hagal's Aett, after the god of the weather. The last eight runes are known as Tyr's Aett, Tyr being the god of war. Somewhat tenuously, Frey's runes relate to love, happiness, sexual fulfillment, and life in general; Hagal's to materialistic progress and power, opportunity, and advancement; and Tyr's to spiritual development and the emotions.

When working on runic spreads, some runes will emerge reversed. When this happens, the message of the rune is either reversed or made more problematic. Some runes, such as Is and Gyfu, cannot be reversed.

HOW TO CAST THE RUNES

When casting the runes, sit calmly and quietly and concentrate on the question or problem in mind. You may like to light a perfumed candle to create a peaceful atmosphere. Take your runes from their bag and spread them on a smooth surface, face down. Carefully move the runes around, in order to "shuffle" them. Then, with your question uppermost in your mind, concentrate on the runes until you feel ready to select the number required for the casting you have decided to use. Place them in one of the ways shown in the diagrams on pages 32–33, making certain that they are placed in the chosen layout in exactly the right order. Having done this, turn each rune over sideways, not top to bottom, in order to show its symbol.

Always take your time when building your interpretation, and follow our basic readings for each rune. See what the runes are telling you and, in addition, pay attention to the overall pattern that emerges from their wisdom. An alternative method of selecting the runes is used by some runic masters: instead of taking all of the runes out face down, as described above, you draw each rune from the bag as required. This is an interesting approach and quite legitimate. It is particularly helpful if, for instance, you are uncertain what to do and need help on a day-to-day matter. Simply put your hand into the bag. The rune that falls into your hand will help you come to your decision.

Memorial Stone

Runic script describing myth and legend was commonly carved onto Norse memorial stones. This stone, believed to date from the 10th century AD, is now in the National Museum in Copenhagen.

HOW TO MAKE THE RUNES

The runes that are supplied in *Parkers' Prediction Pack* are simply cardboard. You can push them out of the sheet and use them just as they are, but the rune masters of the past always made, and encouraged their students to make, their own runes. The runes you make for yourself become very personal you, and seem to react more strongly when you cast them; so kind of psychic bond seems to be forged between you and the

So why not make your own? The material you decide to use is very much up to you. We suggest wood or stone; but you could use glass or plastic disks, or almost any small, round, or oval objects that feel right for you. If using stones, you must find pebbles of a very similar size and appearance. If wood, choose a length which is consistent in its diameter, and saw it into 25 slices of the same thickness. It may be necessary to smooth off and treat each slice with a sealer or matt varnish. In all cases, make sure that the surface of the stone or wood is free of grease or grit.

Paint the rune symbols onto each of the pebbles or pieces of wood. The paint must withstand washing in water, as it is important you are able to clean your runes. You will now have a unique set of runes. Remember that as we include Wyrd, the blank rune (*see page 41*), you will need to keep one stone or slice of wood totally blank. Keep your own runes in a little, soft fabric bag. Add a drawstring to the top so that they will not inadvertently fall out.

THE RUNE CASTINGS

EACH RUNE CASTING IS PARTICULARLY SUITABLE FOR A CERTAIN TYPE OF QUESTION. BEFORE YOU SELECT YOUR RUNES, BE CLEAR IN YOUR OWN MIND WHETHER YOUR QUESTION IS, FOR EXAMPLE, MINOR OR SERIOUS, PRACTICAL OR PSYCHOLOGICAL; THEN CHOOSE YOUR RUNE CASTING ACCORDINGLY. SELECT THE CORRECT NUMBER OF RUNES AND LAY THEM IN THE ORDER SHOWN ON THESE TWO PAGES.

THE 10-RUNE CASTING

The 10-rune casting is a classic. It should only be used when you need a long-term, overall picture of your life as it is at the moment, and require guidance on the correct path to take. Remember that the runes will not tell you what to do, but they will prepare you to come to the decision that you have to make. They are usually reassuring, and should give you the necessary confidence to be bold in your actions. Never consult the 10-rune casting lightly, and do not insult it with a question of minor importance. However, if you are considering serious, life-changing issues such as coping with job loss, ending a long-term relationship, moving, or starting a family, then this is certainly the spread to use.

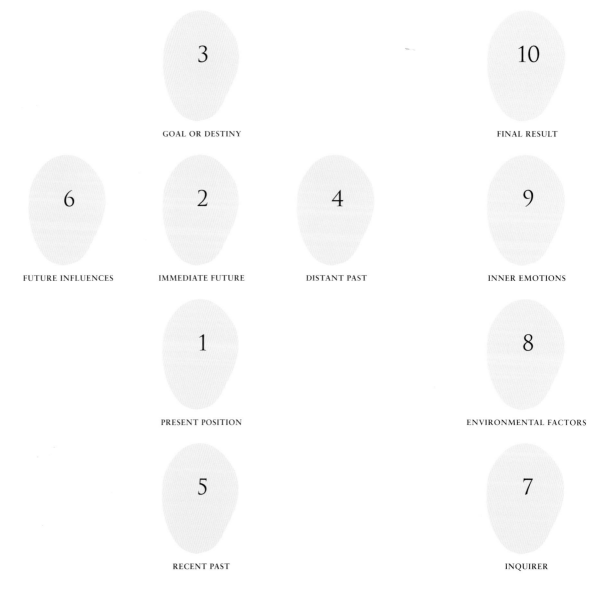

3
GOAL OR DESTINY

10
FINAL RESULT

6
FUTURE INFLUENCES

2
IMMEDIATE FUTURE

4
DISTANT PAST

9
INNER EMOTIONS

1
PRESENT POSITION

8
ENVIRONMENTAL FACTORS

5
RECENT PAST

7
INQUIRER

THE YES/NO CASTING

The Yes/No casting can be used when you have to make a simple decision. Place the runes face down as below. Turn them over once they are all laid out. If a rune is the right way up it receives one point. Rune number 3 is a key rune, and if it is the correct way up it receives two points. If a rune is inverted (upside down), no points are awarded. If the majority of runes are the right way up the answer is yes; if inverted, the answer is no. Count the points. If the total is an even number, the runes are undecided. Some runes look the same either way up – if there are a majority of these in the casting, wait a few days before reaching your decision.

Place stones in the order as numbered

1   2   3   4   5

THE ZODIAC CASTING

There is an age-old mythical relationship between the zodiac and the runes; and in this casting, the placing of the 12 runes derives from the circle of the horoscope. Use the Zodiac casting when you wish to examine your deepest motivations and instinctive reactions. Your response to what the runes have to say will be helpful when you are dogged by uncertainty and a lack of self-confidence. Place 12 runes in a circle starting at the 9 o'clock position (number 1 in the diagram) and contine to place the runes counterclockwise. Each rune represents a particular sphere of your life. Do not rush your interpretation: listen carefully to what each rune has to say, and allow yourself sufficient time to absorb its message.

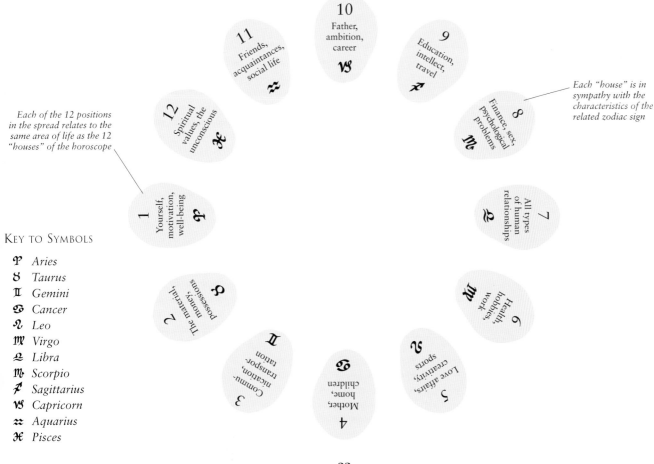

10 Father, ambition, career ♑

11 Friends, acquaintances, social life ♒

9 Education, intellect, travel ♐

12 Spiritual values, the unconscious ♓

8 Finance, sex, psychological problems ♏

Each of the 12 positions in the spread relates to the same area of life as the 12 "houses" of the horoscope

Each "house" is in sympathy with the characteristics of the related zodiac sign

1 Yourself, motivation, well-being ♈

7 All types of human relationships ♎

2 The material, the money, possessions ♉

6 Health, hobbies, work ♍

3 Communication, transport, tuition ♊

4 Mother, home, children ♋

5 Love affairs, creativity, sports ♌

Key to Symbols

♈ *Aries*
♉ *Taurus*
♊ *Gemini*
♋ *Cancer*
♌ *Leo*
♍ *Virgo*
♎ *Libra*
♏ *Scorpio*
♐ *Sagittarius*
♑ *Capricorn*
♒ *Aquarius*
♓ *Pisces*

FREY'S AETT

FEOH

In its historical context Feoh represented cattle, which even from early Egyptian times indicated prosperity. Here we have a powerful link with the zodiac sign Taurus.

What Feoh is telling you

This is a very fortunate rune, associated with all the good things of life and particularly with possessions, property, and a stable and ever-growing bank balance. However, the rune warns against self-indulgence and possessiveness, and tells you to beware of stagnation and allowing yourself to become too set in your ways. It indicates harmony within your relationship, providing you do not consider your loved one as another possession, and encourages you to express yourself through creative work. Feoh also encourages you to take regular exercise, and to watch your intake of rich food. If the rune is reversed, it warns of loss of wealth or other financial difficulties.

KEY WORDS
Harmony, fertility, security.

UR

KEY WORDS
Power, energy, force.

Ur is the symbol of the aurochs, an extinct breed of wild bison that disappeared in the 17th century. Ur is very powerful and represents untamed energy and freedom.

What Ur is telling you

Ur says that you must control and use all your energy – emotional as well as physical – very positively and constructively. Otherwise you tend to be reckless and will fail to gain respect from other people. You will quite rightly be accused of bludgeoning them into what you desire and get the reputation of a bully. You may already be entering a period of inner change and greater self-awareness, and in doing so you will be channeling all your powerful energy in more rewarding directions. Ur advises you to expend excess energy by becoming involved in a demanding sporting activity, especially if your career is sedentary. Reversed, Ur denotes a time of physical or mental weakness.

THORN

Related to the power of the god Thor, a thorn is something to be treated with respect; otherwise it can stab one unmercifully. But, like the thorn on the stem of the rose, it also protects. It is considered a phallic symbol.

What Thorn is telling you

Thorn's boundless energy can be used for good or ill, but you are advised to practice restraint and be circumspect in all your dealings. Consider your next move carefully, especially if other people are involved, since you might be "stabbed in the back." It advises you to negotiate and seek harmony. Rather differently, Thorn is sometimes known as Gateway, and you should consider what might lie at the other side of the gate: a place of peace or some unknown danger? You may be about to move forward psychologically. If so, you must give yourself time for serious thought. If Thorn is reversed it indicates poor decision making or excessive caution.

KEY WORDS
Strength, energy, caution.

ANSUR

KEY WORDS
Wisdom, communication.

Ansur is associated with the Norse god Odin. It is the rune of the spoken word and all types of communication, so is linked to the astrological influence of Mercury. It represents advice, wisdom, and authority of parents and elders.

What Ansur is telling you

Ansur is saying that, as Odin is an old and wise god, you may receive sound advice from an older person that you should take seriously. Your powers of communication are very much improved, and will be useful if you have to deliver a lecture, present your case to other people, or if you have an article to write or an important document to sign. Ansur is associated with learning and understanding, and can indicate a chance meeting with someone who is able to clarify a situation that has been puzzling you. This rune urges you to take any advice that is offered and deliberate before taking action. Reversed, Ansur indicates problems with authority figures.

RAD

Rad is German for wheel. Traditionally, this rune represents either a physical journey to some new location or a spiritual journey. It symbolizes movement and change, and sometimes psychological progress.

What Rad is telling you

Rad tells you to be well prepared for any journey, whether you are about to go off on vacation or you are setting out on a journey of spiritual or psychological discovery. Rad also says that you should not ignore any messages or warnings you receive, and that you should take heed of lessons to be learned from the people and customs you encounter, or from studies relating to your chosen spiritual path. Rad says that now may be the time to take up an intellectual challenge, perhaps the study of a subject that has always interested you. Whatever the nature of your particular journey, as long as you keep the end in sight you cannot lose. If Rad is reversed, it predicts problems with journeys and suggests you take extra care in your arrangements.

KEY WORDS
*Wheels, long journeys –
intellectual or physical.*

KEN

KEY WORDS
Light, creative fire.

Here is the torchbearer of the runes. Ken lights the path ahead of us, creates fiery energy within us, and is sympathetic to the astrological influence of Mars.

What Ken is telling you

Ken's influence must be controlled, but is generally very positive. It will help you to see your present situation far more clearly, and if you allow yourself time for thought, you will clear away any obstacle that is impeding your progress. Ken encourages enthusiasm and optimism. If you are feeling somewhat pessimistic, its lively influence will lighten your burden. Ken is also symbolic of the power of regeneration, and has a bearing on fertility. It is an excellent rune if you are thinking about increasing your family, since it influences passion and sexual desire. Remember that fire is a good servant but a cruel master. Be assertive, but do not become ruthless or impulsive. If Ken is reversed, it can warn the inquirer against a lack of direction or even a lack of warmth toward others.

GYFU

Gyfu means "offerings to the gods" and is the sign of gifts of love and friendship. It is the rune of teamwork and partnership, and is related to the astrological influence of Venus.

What Gyfu is telling you

Although Gyfu is generally associated with matters of the heart, it is not entirely benevolent. Look at Gyfu's symbol. It is a kiss but also a cross. Gyfu tells you of love, friendship, and the possibility of a wonderful partnership, but strongly reminds you that with every partnership comes an element of sacrifice. Remember the saying, "give and take"? It has relevance here. We must be prepared for certain personal sacrifices if we are to make our relationships work. Gifts of love, whether they are spiritual or physical, must be given freely. When Gyfu appears in a spread, it can also be a literal indication that a gift is coming to the inquirer. The gift can be advice, or money, or love. But Gyfu reminds us that there will be a price to pay. Nothing in life is free.

KEY WORDS
Generosity, gifts, love, sacrifice.

WYN

KEY WORDS
Joy, happiness.

Wyn represents the kind of joyous happiness that comes from the feeling of being at one with ourselves, the world, and our own particular god. It symbolizes harmony and inner peace, and those rare moments of balance and calm we all feel at times.

What Wyn is telling you

Wyn is doing its best to help you increase your self-confidence. Perhaps you are far too self-critical, or are listening to those who put you down. Wyn tells you to put such thoughts and remarks behind you, and to think about your past achievements. Even if they are not as good as you would like, they are greater than you imagine. While you should not ignore any difficulties that lie ahead of you, be assured that changes for the better are on the way. The time is right to broaden your horizons and perhaps to relax more. Be hopeful and positive in your outlook: all will be well. If Wyn is reversed, the inquirer will be unable to meet a challenge that is presented to him or her.

HAGAL'S AETT

HAGAL

Hagal is identified with sudden, disruptive hailstorms. Although over fairly quickly, hailstorms are violent while they last and can be very destructive.

What Hagal is telling you

Hagal is telling you to be prepared for sudden storms ahead. Metaphorically speaking, do not go out without your umbrella. You need to be protected at this time, and the best way to achieve protection is to take care of yourself first. Hagal relates to your health as well as to your career and business commitments. Have a medical checkup. If you are feeling under the weather you may need to take vitamins. Like a hailstorm, any setbacks may be dramatic, but they will not be long-lasting. Consider them an inevitable part of life. Detach yourself from your problems. Don't allow yourself to become full of resentment. You will emerge from any struggle with increased understanding and prestige.

KEY WORDS
Setbacks, problems.

NYD

KEY WORDS
Need, necessity.

Nyd's influence is a stern one. It does not let us off lightly; we learn lessons the hard way when under its influence, but we emerge – sometimes feeling we have suffered a great deal – much stronger human beings.

What Nyd is telling you

Nyd is concerned with needs. It often signifies that you feel you lack life's necessities, and it counsels patience in order to attain these needs. Be cautious about any actions you take, and question your own motives. Nyd wonders if you are simply being greedy and reassures you that emotional, spiritual, and material riches are not that far away. But it adds that you must attain them through a soft approach. If dissatisfied with your lot, Nyd tells you that now is not the time to make drastic changes. Patience will be rewarded. Reversed, Nyd suggests you may have acted in a thoughtless or headstrong way and will have to pay the consequences.

IS

The rune Is means ice. Look at its symbol, identical to the letter 'I.' It stands alone; cold and lonely, but independent. Nothing can move in ice; emotions and plans become frozen.

What Is is telling you

Is tells you that you must be prepared for setbacks. You will feel a certain amount of frustration, and, like Nyd, Is's predecessor, this rune advises you to be patient. You may appear cold and distant to those who are, and want to continue to be, close to you. Try to bear this in mind when assessing your present situation. However, as you are likely to be feeling isolated, you may not be aware of the concerns of people around you. Don't be apprehensive about asking for help. If relationships are in question, this rune does not augur well. It suggests that emotions are likely to have gone too cold to be regenerated. Is counsels patience. You must wait for the sun to come and melt the ice.

KEY WORDS
Ice, coldness.

GER

KEY WORDS
Seasons, the natural cycle.

Ger means harvest, but it also represents the cycle of the whole year, from season to season. It relates to your current work, and encourages slow but steady progress. Ger's symbol is like a wheel, and this rune reads the same whichever way it falls.

What Ger is telling you

Ger encourages you to work consistently and hard. You must control the way you spend your time and energy, keeping a balance between work and pleasure. Perseverance will lead to success, and Ger warns against taking shortcuts because they will prove disastrous. Gradual progress, as one season changes to the next, is a distinct possibility at this time; and as it occurs you will be ready for the next new phase. This rune is also connected to justice: a harvest reminds us that we reap what we sow, and Ger says you will gain just rewards for your efforts. Conversely you will be reprimanded for uncharitable actions.

EOH

Eoh means yew, an evergreen tree that is still found in church cemeteries today and is traditionally associated with death. Eoh represents the journeys of the dead. It is related to Odin, the god who accompanied souls to the unseen realms. Do not be apprehensive if you draw this rune.

What Eoh is telling you
Like the thirteenth card of the Tarot's Major Arcana (*see page 15*), there is nothing frightening about Eoh. It does not mean that you or anyone close to you is going to die. Instead, it is a very positive rune. It represents change, the sweeping away of old, worn-out ideas, concepts, and opinions, and says that you are ready to move on. Eoh also suggests that you may be approaching certain goals in your life and will have cause to feel proud of your achievements. You will be particularly successful, especially if other runes in your draw are supportive of this. Remember, too, that as yew trees are evergreen they give hope and are indicative of eternity.

KEY WORDS
Yew tree, journeys of the dead.

PEORTH

KEY WORDS
Mystery, secrecy.

What this rune represents is, in itself, something of a mystery. There is little agreement among runic scholars. It has been described variously as a dice-cup, a chess piece, even a fertility symbol. It has come to symbolize the mystery of the unknown.

What Peorth may be telling you
Peorth suggests that there is an element of secrecy in your life at present. Whether you disclose what is hidden is very much up to you; but before you do you must think carefully. Some interpreters suggest that here, too, is a game of chance: perhaps you have placed a bet or taken a risk. Peorth says that you should make the most of what you have. The rune also has a sexual connotation and might indicate that a pregnancy is soon to happen. It is also linked to the pleasures of food and wine. If you are interested in developing your psychic powers, Peorth gives you its blessing, but advises you to do so with the support of experts. Reversed, Peorth warns that a discomforting secret will be revealed.

EOLH

Eolh is a very powerful and positive rune. It is protective, and indicative of the warding off of evil – the symbol resembles a hand held up as if shielding from danger. This rune can be seen as a protective charm wherever it appears in a rune spread.

What Eolh is telling you
This is a splendid rune. It assures you that you are in a strong and successful position because you have worked hard and achieved a great deal. Life should be enjoyed to the full. There are new challenges around the corner, and you must be ready to accept them with your natural enthusiasm. Eolh indicates that the inquirer is protected from problems and dangers at this time and should take this opportunity to grasp new opportunities. Eolh reminds you to keep your emotions under control, and also advises caution if you are involved with people who like to use others for their own advancement. If Eolh is reversed, it can signify the inquirer has been or will be duped by such unscrupulous people.

KEY WORDS
Defense, protection.

SIGEL

KEY WORDS
Sun, good health, vitality.

Here is the rune of success and happiness. The symbol is one of victory, but can also represent the taking up of arms against evil. This rune represents the sun and is associated with the astrological sign of Leo.

What Sigel is telling you
The vitality and vigor of the sun will now come into play in your life. All your talent and ability will come into prominence, and you will reap the fruits of success. This will lead to happiness and contentment. However, you should not rest on your laurels for too long. Think about your next phase or project. Aim to make use of and further develop your full potential. Your vision is clear, and you can at once see what is right for yourself and your loved ones. Sigel's warnings are that you might take on too much, or be involved in too many tasks at the same time. You also need to avoid showing off and overdramatic behavior. Spiritually, Sigel represents the power of light over darkness; if you are searching for spiritual guidance, you will find it soon.

TYR'S AETT

TYR

Traditionally known as the warrior rune, Tyr symbolizes courage and dedication and is sympathetic to the astrological influence of Mars. Tyr is related to the Greek god Zeus and the Roman god Jupiter.

What Tyr is telling you

Tyr indicates that a battle may be about to ensue, and that you will need lots of physical and mental energy. Tyr recommends that you cultivate patience, and reminds you to abide by the rules of justice and fairness. It encourages self-reliance, determination, and an uncomplicated approach to problems. Tyr is the symbol of male sexuality, saying that with pure passion comes happiness. It recommends you to take positive action, as you will then gain respect from other people. It urges you to go forward with confidence to achieve what you most desire. Reversed, Tyr suggests that the inquirer may be feeling mentally or physically weak.

KEY WORDS
Courage, combat, justice.

BEORC

KEY WORDS
Birth, new beginnings, renewal.

Beorc is the rune of the home and family. Here we also have an accent on regeneration, renewal, all forms of healing, fertility, and the pleasure of sexual relationships.

What Beorc is telling you

Beorc says that if you have thoughts of starting or increasing a family, the time is right to do so. If considering buying a new home or making alterations to your existing one, go ahead. However, Beorc also represents a spiritual birth – or rebirth. If you are thinking of returning to some neglected skill or interest, you will make good progress. This rune is supportive if you are about to embark on a new enterprise. It may also be that you have "seen the light" in a spiritual sense, in which case Beorc will help you along your new path to enlightenment. If Beorc appears reversed it can denote domestic problems or illness, but it is not malign in itself. Surrounding runes will clarify the situation.

EHWAZ

Ehwaz is the rune of travel, and it also represents the horse and the relationship that exists between a horse and its rider. Ehwaz refers to the importance of partnership, trust, faith, and loyalty.

What Ehwaz is telling you

Here is the opportunity for material and spiritual advancement. There is an accent on controlled change and on partnership, so should opportunities occur that require you to change direction in life, Ehwaz advises you to consider them carefully and discuss them with your partner, or perhaps a brother or sister; ensure that he or she approves of any change and continues to support you. It is possible that you will travel in the near future. This will be rewarding and perhaps lucrative – even if your trip is an expensive one! If Ehwaz is reversed it still suggests a journey, but maybe one that is made out of necessity rather than choice.

KEY WORDS
Horse, partnership, advancement.

MAN

KEY WORDS
Intelligence, culture.

Man represents the human race as a whole and not simply the male members of the species. The rune stands for intelligence, culture, and all human characteristics. It reminds us that while we are part of the human race, we each stand alone.

What Man is telling you

Man advises you to take a broad perspective before making any judgment, that you should keep your life in balance by not reacting over-emotionally, and that you must respect your body – not abuse it with alcohol, drugs, or excessive dieting. As you are part of the family of the human race, you must preserve and conserve the good things of life and what the planet has to offer. Man advises you to re-examine your attitudes to make sure that your judgment is fair and unbiased. Reversed, Man suggests that your problems may well be of your own making, and that you need to cooperate more with others.

LAGU

Lagu is related to flowing water and thus symbolizes our emotions and unconscious. It suggests fluidity and change, imagination and intuition, but also lack of control.

What Lagu is telling you

Although water is essential to life, you need to be careful not to drown in it. Lagu advises you not to become so emotional that you lose your rational and practical outlook. Alternatively, when Lagu appears in a rune spread, it can indicate the reverse – that you have suppressed your emotions and are appearing hard or indifferent to those who love you, and who you love. Being aware of either of these possibilities is crucial to your development as a human being. Lagu also reminds you that you should be flexible in your opinions, be in control of your intuition, and to express psychic or creative talent. Lagu advises you not to ignore your innermost feelings. If reversed, Lagu suggests that your intuition is not to be trusted. You would be wise to take advice from others.

KEY WORDS
Water, the unconscious, emotion.

ING

KEY WORDS
Fertility, conclusion, completion.

Ing represents the completion of a project or the conclusion of some event or period in our lives. It is also indicative of someone who is expressing their full potential and is satisfied that they are taking the right course of action. Ing is commonly associated with fertility, family, and the home.

What Ing is telling you

Ing says that having made certain decisions you can now relax, assured that you are on the right path. Your mind should now be free of worry and you no longer have any cause for concern. This rune is important because it is thought to indicate that you have finally completed one particular phase of your life and can now look forward to the next phase with renewed confidence, having gained vital experience by living through previous events. Ing's appearance in a spread is also positive because it represents fertility and birth, a secure home and family life. On a spiritual level, it suggests the inquirer will soon find inner peace and calm.

DAEG

Daeg means day, and this rune symbolizes the day dawning after the dark night. In the long Nordic winters the dawning of a new day was confirmation of life and growth. Daeg represents light after dark, the dawn of new ideas, and a period of growth in life, including spiritual development.

What Daeg is telling you

Daeg tells you to expect some transformation that will be to your advantage. This rune is a very positive one to appear in a rune spread. It says that good times are on the way and any darkness you may have experienced through grief or depression is over. You will achieve what you desire, and your finances will be more stable than previously. Be confident – you have no need to be otherwise, since now you are in a period of growth and progress. Daeg's one warning is that you should guard against recklessness; it suggests you nurture your new enlightenment with periods of quiet reflection or meditation. You now have a great deal to offer others.

KEY WORDS
Day, awakening.

ODEL

KEY WORDS
Inherited property, ancestors.

Odel, sometimes known as Epel, represents home and family traditions; shared rapport; family money and land; love and affection – or rifts and quarrels. Odel reminds us of our inheritance and our ancestors. It also has a bearing on beginnings and endings.

What Odel is telling you

Odel focuses on family ties and traditions, and warns against a severance of these bonds and relationships. Such breaks are likely to be long-lasting and very important to you and the other people concerned. Your present situation could be difficult, but it is vital that you realize you are unlikely to make a serious mistake. Any hurt will be painful, but eventually you will know that you did the right thing at the right time and will feel reborn. Odel's influence also covers inherited personality traits and appearance, and this rune reminds you of the importance of your family. If Odel is reversed, it says you can expect no help from others with what lies ahead. A coming battle must be fought alone.

RUNES – A CASE HISTORY

GUIDED BY THE AUTHORS, THE INQUIRER, MICHELLE, CHOSE THE 10-RUNE CASTING FOR HER QUESTION BECAUSE IT OFFERS THE ADDITIONAL DETAIL THAT WILL HELP HER TO REACH HER DECISION. THE 10-RUNE CASTING PROVIDES AN OVERVIEW OF YOUR LIFE AS IT IS AT THE MOMENT, AND OFFERS GUIDANCE ON THE RIGHT PATH TO FOLLOW. IT SHOULD ONLY BE USED FOR MAJOR ISSUES.

THE BACKGROUND

Michelle and Andrew have a son, James. They have carefully considered James' move to secondary education, and have decided that they would like him to go to a private school. Although the school has an excellent reputation, James has flatly refused to go. When his parents asked him to at least take the entrance examination, he threatened to deliberately do badly in order to fail. He wishes to attend the local school, which has a good reputation, even though the facilities are unimpressive. His parents feel that James would not reach his full potential at this school. Michelle asked the runes: "Should we allow James to go to the school of his choice, or should we force him to abide by our wishes?"

3. GOAL OR DESTINY

10. FINAL RESULT

6. FUTURE INFLUENCES

2. IMMEDIATE FUTURE

4. DISTANT PAST

9. INNER EMOTIONS

1. PRESENT POSITION

8. ENVIRONMENTAL FACTORS

5. RECENT PAST

7. INQUIRER

OVERALL LOOK AT THE SPREAD

Here is a brief summary of the spread. We suggest that you read the full interpretation of each rune, on pages 34-39, as you go through this shortened interpretation. The 10-rune casting was considered the most suitable spread for answering Michelle's very serious question. There were only two inverted runes (Lagu in position three and Man in position five) in the casting. This infers that there will not be too much delay in the resolution of Michelle's problem.

1. PRESENT POSITION

Sigel. The Sun, good health, and vitality. The rune of happiness and success. But at this stage in the interpretation we do not know whether James or his parents will win the argument. Because the rune is of such a positive nature it seems that a happy resolution will be the eventual outcome.

2. IMMEDIATE FUTURE

Ehwaz. Loyalty, travel, a spiritual journey, and a living, vibrant partnership. This is indicative of the very close and lively relationship James has with his parents. He gets all the support and love possible. There is an accent on controlled change and the advice that everything should be discussed in detail. The journey mentioned in the full interpretation of this rune here represents James' journey through his school days.

3. GOAL OR DESTINY

Lagu (inverted). Lagu is warning Michelle that she must not allow her emotions to overcome her. She needs to be practical when making her decision, but also flexible and aware of other people's opinions.

4. DISTANT PAST

Ur. Here power, force, and energy are represented. Ur refers quite clearly to the position James has been taking, reflecting on the fact that he was bludgeoning his parents into what he most desires.

5. RECENT PAST

Man (inverted). The rune shows that Michelle is taking a broad perspective before coming to her decision. She has been, as the rune suggests, aiming not to react overemotionally. Man advises cooperation and hints that perhaps she is making too much of her problem.

6. FUTURE INFLUENCES

Peorth. Here secrecy is hinted at, as is risk-taking. Perhaps Michelle should delve more deeply into James' deep-rooted psychological reasons, to encourage him to reveal what he is hiding.

7. INQUIRER

Ger. Ger is representing Michelle. She does, in fact, work hard and consistently for her husband and son, and for many good causes. As justice is represented in this rune, she can be confident that her and her husband's eventual decision will be the right one.

8. ENVIRONMENTAL FACTORS

Thorn. Thorn encourages Michelle to be circumspect and to consider her every action carefully. As environmental issues are presented here, it supports her constant thoughts on her son's reaction to the very different atmospheres, environments, and objectives of the schools in question. In the full interpretation (*see page 34*), the mention of what lies at the other side of the gate indicates that the eventual decision will take James along one of two very different paths.

9. INNER EMOTIONS

Nyd. Michelle must be patient. Nyd's message is that she must attain her objective by a gentle approach. There is no point in trying to force the issue with James. She must also be prepared for delays.

10. FINAL RESULT

Rad. The indication of a long journey – another reference to James' years of education ahead. It seems that neither James nor his parents will lose with this very appropriate rune placed at the "final result" position. Michelle will be able to pass on Rad's message in simple terms to James. The rune is, in fact, full of suggestions – albeit somewhat oblique ones – which will help James to see his parents' point of view and hopefully become more open-minded.

WYRD – THE BLANK RUNE

Many runic masters ignore this rune, which is not part of the most ancient tradition. It represents fate. When Wyrd appears in a spread, it suggests that you have come to a crossroads. It does not indicate which new path you should take, but suggests that you pause and reflect. Allow other runes in your casting to help you, but know that the final decision rests with you. Perhaps you are about to take a step into the unknown – again more thought is needed. A minor incident could prove an important turn of fate for you, although you may well only realize this in retrospect.

I CHING

THE *I CHING* IS AN ANCIENT CHINESE SYSTEM OF DIVINATION CONSISTING OF A SET OF 64 SYMBOLS, KNOWN AS HEXAGRAMS, MADE UP OF BROKEN (YIN) AND UNBROKEN (YANG) HORIZONTAL LINES IN VARYING COMBINATIONS. THE TEXT USED TO INTERPRET THE HEXAGRAMS IS ALSO CALLED THE *I CHING*, OR *BOOK OF CHANGES*.

Confucius and the I Ching
Confucius (Kong Qiu), 550–478 BC, is shown here consulting the I Ching. *He was one of many Chinese historical figures to be involved with the* I Ching.

THE *I CHING* CONTAINS PROFOUND MEANINGS APPLICABLE TO DAILY LIFE. AS A DIVINATION SYSTEM, IT HAS BEEN USED FOR MANY CENTURIES TO offer advice, and to foretell what may happen in any situation. It is founded on the philosophy that yin (the female, passive principle) and yang (the male, active principle) explain all being, and that the world is in a continual state of change – in particular, with the male and female principles interacting – yin becoming yang and vice versa. The *I Ching* offers a symbolic picture of the present, and suggests what will or may happen when the picture changes.

The sets of three yin (broken) and yang (unbroken) lines that make up the body of the *I Ching* – known as trigrams – were said to have been discovered by the legendary figure Fu Hsi around 3000 BC as markings on the back of a tortoise shell; but the text itself was written by a feudal lord, Wen Wang. In 1144 BC, Wen Wang was captured and imprisoned by Emperor Chou Hsin. During his captivity he studied the eight trigrams, and compiled 64 hexagrams – patterns of six lines made up from the eight trigrams. Wen Wang's son, Tan, expanded his father's work and added his own commentary to every line of the hexagrams. In the fifth century BC, the philosopher Confucius added to the commentaries. The result of these centuries of study and contemplation is the *I Ching* or *Book of Changes* – a book that some people claim can explain and even control future events.

Each single line of the 64 hexagrams of the *I Ching* can change from yin to yang, or vice versa. When lines change, this affects the hexagram, which in turn changes into another. Each hexagram as a whole, and each line of the hexagram, is accompanied by poetic images and verses that are applied to the question asked. In the original text, the lines and patterns are often difficult to interpret and apply, especially by a modern reader unaware of Chinese history, mythology, and poetry. To 21st-century Western readers, lines such as:

"His nose and feet are cut off.
Oppression at the hands of the man with the purple knee bands.
Joy comes softly."

from hexagram 47, K'un, line 5 (*I Ching*, tr. Richard Wilhelm, London, Routledge & Kegan Paul, 1951), are difficult to apply. The authors of this book have gone to the root meanings of the lines and simplified them; they will still be found to supply very apt responses to the questions asked.

THROWING THE COINS

The three coins in this pack are based on a genuine Chinese coin. Make the coins particularly your own by washing them in running water, and carrying them around with you – perhaps in a little bag made or bought especially for the purpose.

When you want to consult the *I Ching*, find a quiet area where you will not be disturbed. Take out the coins and hold them in your hands for a moment while you concentrate your mind on your question. You might find it aids your focus to write down your question before you throw the coins. Make your question as simple as possible, but avoid asking for a simple "yes" or "no" answer. Then throw the coins six times onto a flat surface, keeping your question uppermost in your mind as you throw, and noting how the coins fall: the inscribed side is the yin or feminine side, and the blank side is the yang or masculine side. Like a house being built from the foundation, a hexagram is built from the bottom line up: your first throw reveals the bottom line of the six, and so on until your last throw gives the sixth, top line.

When you are starting to use the *I Ching*, it is best to write down the "score" each time you throw. When the coins fall, the blank side (yang) scores 3, and the inscribed side (yin) scores 2. A total score of 7 produces an unbroken line ——, while 8 produces a broken line — —. These lines are called Young Yang and Young Yin. Total scores of 6 and 9, made up of three yin or three yang throws respectively, also produce broken and unbroken lines, but these are called Old Yin and Old Yang, and are known as changing or moving lines. A hexagram with changing lines indicates that a second hexagram has to be constructed. No coins have to be thrown for the second hexagram. Instead, it is simply a case of "changing" the lines to their complementary opposite: Old Yin becomes Young Yang (a broken line becomes an unbroken line), and Old Yang become Young Yin (an unbroken line becomes a broken line).

THE COINS AND THE LINES

COIN	PRINCIPLE	SCORE
	Yin	2
	Yang	3

The Coins
The universe is encapsulated in these Chinese coins: the round shape represents heaven, while the square hole in the middle represents earth.

SCORE	LINE	NAME
6	—x—	*Old Yin*
7	——	*Young Yang*
8	— —	*Young Yin*
9	—o—	*Old Yang*

The Lines
Scores of 7 and 8 give static lines (Young Yang and Young Yin), but scores of 6 and 9 give lines that change to their complementary opposite: Old Yin changes to Young Yang, and Old Yang changes to Young Yin.

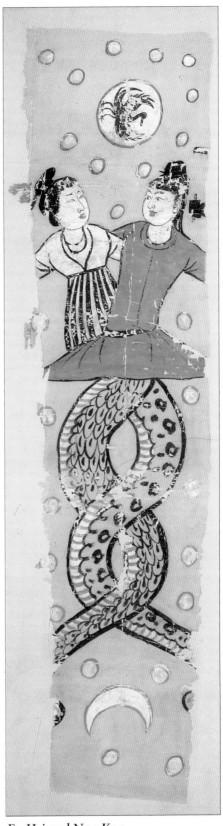

Fu Hsi and Nua Kua
This 7th-century silk painting shows the legendary Chinese ruler Fu Hsi (right), entwined with his successor, Nua Kua. Fu Hsi is said to have discovered the eight trigrams on the back of a tortoise shell.

CONSULTING THE I CHING

IT IS REMARKABLE HOW THE *I CHING* INVARIABLY HAS SOMETHING RELEVANT TO SAY ABOUT ANY QUESTION ASKED – THOUGH DO NOT EXPECT EVERY SINGLE LINE TO HAVE A BEARING ON YOUR SPECIFIC PROBLEM. NEVERTHELESS, GIVE EVERY LINE PROPER CONSIDERATION, FOR SOMETIMES THE COMMENT IS OBLIQUE. NEVER ASK THE *I CHING* QUESTIONS FOR FUN – ALWAYS TREAT IT WITH RESPECT.

The Universal Mirror
The I Ching *was designed to mirror the universe. It often speaks of the changes in the natural world, such as the seasons.*

The Bagua
This 1915 illustration shows the trigrams with the yin/yang symbol in the middle – an arrangement known as the bagua.

THE TRIGRAMS AND THE HEXAGRAMS

Every hexagram consists of two trigrams. It is not accidental that each trigram has its own name and nature, contributing to the effect of the hexagram and its application to your question. The lower trigram, made up of the bottom three lines – the result of your first three throws of the coins – comments on the psychological situation, or how you subjectively view the problem. The top trigram, made up of the top three lines – the result of your last three throws of the coins – comments on the outward situation, how the outside world may see it, and how you must approach it on a purely practical level.

After you have consulted the *I Ching* and have constructed your hexagram, look it up in the Trigrams and Hexagrams Chart on page 45. Find the top three lines of your hexagram in the "Upper Trigram" horizontal row, and the bottom three lines of your hexagram in the "Lower Trigram" vertical column. The square where the trigrams intersect gives the number of the hexagram. For example, the upper trigram Kên and the lower trigram K'an intersect at square 4, which corresponds to hexagram No. 4, Mêng, Youthful Folly.

Turning to the page in this book where your hexagram is interpreted, first look at the two trigrams separately. The Image and The Judgment paragraphs give a general shorthand indication of the trigrams' relevance, based on traditional images – of earth (solidity, dependability), heaven (spirituality), thunder (anger, irrationality), water (indecision, immutability), mountain (difficulty), wind/wood (vacillation), fire (impetuosity), and lake (calmness).

After you have considered the Image and Judgment paragraphs, examine the lines of the hexagram. These six lines are interpreted one by one, with, as always, line 1 being the bottom line and line 6 the top line. If your hexagram has any changing lines (Old Yin and/or Old Yang), pay particular attention to them. Think of the hexagram as commenting on the situation at the time when the question is being asked. A hexagram with no changing lines indicates that the situation is as shown in the commentaries of the *I Ching*, and that it is unlikely to change significantly in the near future.

If your hexagram has any changing lines, re-draw the hexagram, turning the changing lines to their complementary opposite: Old Yin to Young Yang (broken line to unbroken line) and Old Yang to Young Yin (unbroken line to broken line). Find the new hexagram in the Trigrams and Hexagrams Chart on page 45, and look up the interpretation. Think of the new hexagram as showing the future: but a future to which you would need to contribute. It shows you not what will be, but what may be, as the result of actions you take after carefully considering the consequences. Note that all of the lines are static – there are never any changing lines in a new hexagram.

ACHIEVEMENT OF A GOAL

As a demonstration, one of the authors consulted the *I Ching* to ask how the work on this pack would progress. The throws of the coins produced scores of 8, 8, 9, 7, 7, 8 (reading from the bottom to the top). The third score from bottom, 9, was produced by three yang throws, which meant that the third line was Old Yang (unbroken) and would change to Young Yin (broken). The scores of the throws produced the trigram Tui at the top and Kên at the bottom, which makes up hexagram No. 31, Hsein, Courtship (see the Trigrams and Hexagrams Chart, below). When the third line was changed from unbroken to broken, the lower trigram changed to K'un, giving the new hexagram No. 45, Ts'ui, Uniting.

As a matter of interest, the interpretation of No. 31, Hsein, Courtship (*see page 61*) emphasizes the attraction between two people (the authors are husband and wife) and the importance of listening to each other. It also speaks of the joint use of instinct and experience, and of thinking of the affect of one's work on one's listeners or readers.

The interpretation of the new hexagram, No. 45, Ts'ui, Uniting (*see page 68*) goes on to insist on the importance of working together to deal with areas of difficulty, though one person must finally make a decision when one is working as part of a team. All of this applies perfectly to the process of producing a book, which is not only written by two people, but edited and designed by a team.

At first, consulting the *I Ching* may seem to be a complicated process, but it really is not – it simply requires a quiet place and a little practice. If you would like to see some more examples of consulting the *I Ching* before you ask a question yourself, turn to the case histories (*see pages 78–79*), which give a detailed background to the question, a step-by-step illustration of the throws of the coins and their scores, and a thorough interpretation of the resulting hexagrams.

Man or Myth?
In some ancient Chinese texts, Fu Hsi is described as part human and part animal; but here he is depicted in human form, holding the bagua.

CHART OF NUMBERS AND TRIGRAMS

UPPER TRIGRAM ▶ / LOWER TRIGRAM ▼	CH'IEN	CHÊN	K'AN	KÊN	K'UN	SUN	LI	TUI
CH'IEN	1	34	5	26	11	9	14	43
CHÊN	25	51	3	27	24	42	21	17
K'AN	6	40	29	4	7	59	64	47
KÊN	33	62	39	52	15	53	56	31
K'UN	12	16	8	23	2	20	35	45
SUN	44	32	48	18	46	57	50	28
LI	13	55	63	22	36	37	30	49
TUI	10	54	60	41	19	61	38	58

THE HEXAGRAMS

1 CH'IEN ~ *The Creative*

This extremely strong hexagram, with its two blocks of unbroken lines, suggests that you have the strength to cope with the situation with which you are faced. You should not forget the psychological aspects of the problem, but essentially it is the sheer strength of your mind and personality that will enable you to cope.

The Judgment
You are undoubtedly strong, but it would be an error to take other people's strength for granted. Test each step of the ladder before you put your weight on it. And in taking those steps, do not elbow others out of the way; be considerate.

The Image
The Chinese verse reminds us that as time passes, situations inevitably change; it is up to you to seek reality and take a stance that enables you to remain consistent and true to yourself during changing circumstances. Conserve your energy – both physical and psychological – very carefully.

The Lines
1 Your energy is like a hidden dragon, waiting to startle the world with its dynamic, creative, and timely force. Keep it concealed until the time is ripe.

2 Work together with friends or colleagues. Keep your place in the pattern – that way your strength and determination will best be used. Don't be afraid of accepting advice.

3 When push comes to shove, you will be the one with the strength to keep going. Don't let others distract you, and don't view difficulties as intractable – they're not.

4 When the dust settles, you can continue to play an important part, or withdraw and let others carry on. Your decision will be correct.

5 Your problem-solving will be applauded, others will admire you and ask for your help. But responsibility can be lonely work.

6 Don't lose touch with reality just because you have been successful in problem-solving. Remember that pride comes before a fall.

ABOVE: **Ch'ien**
creativity, heaven, strength

BELOW: **Ch'ien**
creativity, heaven, strength

2 K'UN ~ *The Flexible*

ABOVE: **K'un**
flexibility, earth, adaptability

BELOW: **K'un**
flexibility, earth, adaptability

This hexagram, composed of entirely broken yin lines, represents the depths of the female psyche. It is associated with Mother Earth – female rather than masculine, earth rather than heaven. It encourages you to listen, to understand, and to immerse yourself thoroughly in a problem or situation so that you know it from the inside out. Be open in your responses, and trust your intuition.

The Judgment
The Chinese image is that of a mare, swift and sturdy but also gentle and devoted. The mare is full of life and vitality, naturally powerful, tireless in pursuit of its aim, and able to be guided by others. Consequently, a chief suggestion is to allow yourself to be guided by those you trust, and lend them your strength.

The Image
This hexagram speaks of endless time and space, inviting you to put no boundaries on your consideration of the problem, either because it may appear intractable or because you find any aspect of it repulsive. Don't recoil from the situation – it is only by learning to weigh up the bad as well as the good that you will be able to progress.

The Lines
1 Steel yourself for winter – that is, for a long and cold time. If you protect delicate plants by care and nurture, they survive. Look for signs of storm, and be prepared.

2 Don't waste your energy fighting against the inevitable. Try to accept even the most unpleasant experience. Nature tolerates everything and deals with it in its own way. So must you.

3 Don't thrust yourself forward and shout. Consider the situation, make a forward-looking decision, then act on it – but steadily, quietly, and modestly.

4 It is very probably not yet the time to act. Keep your thoughts to yourself and don't try to persuade others. Watch for developments and add them to your store of knowledge.

5 The original Chinese interpretation speaks of "a yellow undergarment," symbolic of reliability and good fortune. But it also suggests concealment.

6 It is highly likely that there will be trouble, maybe even violence, and everyone will probably get hurt in some way. But few victories are won without casualties.

3 CHUN ~ *Initial Problem*

The combinations of thunder and water, together with danger and an abyss, suggest a very difficult and perilous situation. In Chinese, the name of the hexagram indicates a blade of grass growing with such immense force that it manages to emerge even through concrete. Undoubtedly a difficult start; but remember that although a thunderstorm is noisy and possibly frightening, it clears the air of tension and stagnation, and is often followed by freshness and calm.

The Judgment

If one blade of grass is growing, so is the whole of nature; and out of difficulty success will inevitably come, probably with the help of others. Premature or careless action will be dangerous and provoke attacks. So tread carefully at all times.

The Image

More indication of early difficulty and muddle, and perhaps even anarchy. However, order is within the situation; but you must seek it out, and through careful early planning, lay down a clear path to follow. Try to regard difficulties as positively goading you to a solution. Once more, avoid premature action.

The Lines

1 If you are confronted with a difficulty, stop and think, but don't be thrown off course. Seek out the right people to help you forward. Ask them nicely, and don't reject advice because you disagree with it.

2 A very sudden incident will help solve the problem. Don't be suspicious, even if the unexpected seems unhelpful. But don't place yourself under too great an obligation.

3 Don't force things. Ask for help – from friends, family, colleagues, God if you will – but above all, don't rush in and make things worse by premature action.

4 You need to take action, but you may think you lack the ability. Force yourself to take the first step, even if it is a tentative one, and don't be afraid to accept help from others.

5 Other people are likely to misunderstand and misinterpret your actions, and suspect your motives. Avoid contention and press steadily ahead; difficulties will disappear.

6 Accept that some difficulties are just too great to be faced alone. But don't give up, even in the face of apparent disaster – resignation is no solution.

ABOVE: **K'an**
the abyss, water, danger

BELOW: **Chên**
exhilaration, thunder, provocation

4 MÊNG ~ *Youthful Folly*

Water that bubbles at the foot of a mountain cannot climb – an inexperienced youth should not take on too great a task. Similarly, there is not a great deal to be said for resting when danger – perhaps an abyss – must be overcome. However, it is worth remembering that resting renews strength and that the slow, inexorable drip of water can eventually wear away a surface as hard and unrelenting as granite.

The Judgment

The vigor and energy of youth can be triumphant given proper guidance – and the young must realize that they need the wisdom and sagacity of the experienced. It is important to seek out the right adviser. If you are asked for advice, make sure that it is clear, short, sharp, and succinct – not tentative or muddled.

The Image

A spring does not collect in stale pools – it remains fresh and full of vitality through natural movement. Move continually forward in life, and learn many new lessons. Be open and thorough in your life experience – pay attention at all times and allow no useful message to be ignored.

The Lines

1 Life is real and life is earnest: have you been taking it too lightly? Learn discipline – but not to the extent of ceasing to be flexible.

2 You are strong and tolerant enough to be able to suffer fools – if not gladly, at least without bigotry. Inner strength combined with forbearance equips you for peacemaking.

3 Don't slavishly act on other people's advice without thinking things through, or give in to someone who has a stronger personality than you. Give your trust grudgingly.

4 Don't take the easy way out by donning rose-colored glasses, ignoring reality, or seeing things not as they are but as you would have them. A dream may be pleasant, but it is always only a dream.

5 Be childlike in your approach to a teacher you trust: once trust has been earned, give it completely and unquestioningly. The truth may hurt, but it is still the truth.

6 Sometimes you simply have to punish foolishness, if merely by showing it up. If you have to act, do so with reason and kindness. Your own foolishness, once revealed, should be admitted at once.

ABOVE: **Kên**
obduracy, mountain, rest

BELOW: **K'an**
the abyss, water, danger

5 HSÜ ~ Waiting

Here, inner strength is used to combat external danger. The wise man or woman waits calmly, preserving his or her strength for the test that is to come – or for the danger to pass. The hexagram also relates to the clouds from which nourishing rain falls onto the parched earth. The best course of action is to wait patiently – the solution to a problem may come as unexpectedly as a refreshing summer shower.

The Judgment

Here there is water, danger, and an abyss; but an inventive mind together with inner confidence and physical strength will enable you to cross them safely. A clear view and understanding of your objectives should help to achieve your aims.

The Image

There is absolutely no need to allow apprehension, worry, and anxiety to affect or even ruin your life. Be positive – eat, drink, and be merry instead. Remember that a relaxed and well-fed body and mind are most useful to you in trying times. Have confidence in yourself, and believe that you will be ready to meet any emergency which eventually presents itself.

The Lines

1 "Something's coming." You cannot guess what, but there is a stirring in the air. Don't try to guess what may be ahead. Carry on as usual, calmly and without fear.

2 Remain calm, and don't blame anyone else if your life and prospects seem uncertain. Your future is in your own hands, but bide your time.

3 Sand and mud make your footsteps heavy, hampering your progress. Enemies may seem to take advantage of this. Recognize your vulnerability and work out your defense.

4 You seem isolated, and in some sort of a trap. Don't panic and flounder around – you will only make matters worse. Stand still and accept whatever is coming.

5 In any dangerous position there are always moments of calm: take advantage of them. Be sure of your basic position, and feel confident. No one can shake you if you remain composed.

6 The waiting is over. Does everything seem to have been in vain? Be patient – something unexpected will happen. Treat this with care; rescue may be in sight.

ABOVE: **K'an**
the abyss, water, danger

BELOW: **Ch'ien**
creativity, heaven, strength

6 SUNG ~ Strife

ABOVE: **Ch'ien**
creativity, heaven, strength

BELOW: **K'an**
the abyss, water, danger

Heaven is above, the abyss is below; water falls from one to the other. The basic idea at work here is one of separation, even antagonism. Creativity might overcome this, perhaps by the use of stealth and cunning, which again may give rise to a certain amount of friction. The hexagram's essential emotion is apprehension – of some trial ahead that is more than likely to give you some unsettling moments in the future.

The Judgment

If you are in the right, then all is well and you can relax. If you are in the wrong, resist the temptation to indulge in any devious or underhanded behavior. Keep a clear, honest head at all times, and work out a way of backing down from the situation without any great loss of face.

The Image

There is an almost instinctive antagonism in the situation; and once this shows itself, opposition seems inevitable. Think through the situation slowly and methodically. Carefully examine the possibility of keeping the conflicting elements apart – this enforced separation might remove the cause before the effect can follow.

The Lines

1 It's not worth pushing things. Accept that you may have to lose a battle in order to win the war. There may be trouble, but things will finally turn out to your advantage.

2 Refuse to take part in an unequal struggle. Far better to give ground, rethink your position, and take the line of least resistance in order to achieve real benefit.

3 Know your own worth. Knowledge, wisdom, and understanding come through any experience – so embrace it, and the vision that comes from it, thoroughly.

4 You may be in a stronger position than an antagonist, but in the end you cannot triumph unless you are in the right. Accept what your conscience tells you.

5 If you are in the right, make sure that others hear you. If someone else is the arbiter and you respect their judgment, accept their decision – even if it surprises or perhaps even offends you.

6 You are in the right, and everyone accepts the fact and gives in to you. But are you happy? Seek a position that satisfies your inner self as well as your sense of justice.

7 SHIH ~ *The Army*

Water is stored up in the ground, ready for use, in the same way that the population is available as a source of military strength. This is a disturbing and uneasy combination of trigrams traditionally associated with danger. Here, the danger may be withstood provided there is discipline – as in a fort attacked by threatening insurgents, or an army that may revolt unless properly controlled by a good leader.

The Judgment
An unruly mob can become a force for good if it is controlled by a strong-minded individual; its force should be used sparingly and justly, and only when every other possibility has been explored. The motives for using force should be clearly explained, otherwise strength of purpose and unity will be sadly lacking.

The Image
Although water is invisible, it is necessary to the well-being of the earth. Therefore the hexagram is positive. But just as water must be carefully channeled, so physical power should be kept under control. When physical power has had its effect, it should be quickly replaced by care and nurture.

The Lines
1 Make sure that the cause for which you are fighting is just before you apply any pressure. Be certain that your forces are under firm control and are properly organized.

2 Share any hardships that you must inflict on others. In the end you will be praised for your intervention, but don't allow yourself to be too proud. Remember that the achievement is not all yours.

3 If someone is allowed to interfere with what you have planned, and especially if a group of people try to take over, the result may be disastrous.

4 You may be forced to decide that there is nothing to be done: the forces against you are simply too strong. Indulging in a hopeless struggle will get you nowhere.

5 Indiscipline can only lead to chaos, defeat, and a great deal of pain. Control that is informed by experience can prevent you from making very serious mistakes.

6 Victory. But make sure it is the victory of the just. Do not allow those who do not deserve the credit to take over and profit from the effort and hard work of others.

ABOVE: **K'un**
flexibility, earth, adaptability

BELOW: **K'an**
the abyss, water, danger

8 PI ~ *Partnership*

ABOVE: **K'an**
the abyss, water, danger

BELOW: **K'un**
flexibility, earth, adaptability

Water embraces the earth. It also lies conveniently in hollows, and streams run within channels. The hexagram suggests that you should conform to the disciplines of the society in which you live, guided perhaps by a personality you respect, whose authority over you is justified.

The Judgment
It is very often necessary to work with others, under the authority of one person who can hold the team together. Common experiences strengthen ties and bonds, and latecomers might find it difficult to gain entry. Once you have joined a team, you should give unstinting support. If you cannot, you should leave – but remember that a loner without support has a difficult task.

The Image
Water fills all the empty places on earth, and a healthy society keeps itself together by allowing everyone to feel a member of a larger whole. A stream once in contact with another stream unites with it and becomes stronger. Like-minded people who work together have greater strength than individuals. But make sure every personality becomes part of the group effort.

The Lines
1 Complete openness within a relationship is the only recipe for success. Equivocation is always a mistake. Say what you mean, and mean what you say.

2 It is rarely a good idea to agree with others merely to curry favor with them. Be careful in your response to other people; consider their words and actions, and only follow them if they are convincing.

3 React pleasantly to those who are pleasant with you. But do not plunge into intimacy before you are quite sure that there is a common bond, and one that will last.

4 Be ready to give open support to someone you are convinced is in the right. Do not waver – once you have made the decision to champion a cause, stick to it.

5 Someone asks for your support. They will listen attentively to your advice, even if they fail to act on it. Feel free to speak as frankly as you wish.

6 Are you sure that the first step you have taken is the right one? If it is, the rest will follow – and indeed if you hesitate, a fine opportunity may be lost.

9 HSIAO CH'U ~ *Insignificance*

Small is not only beautiful; it is stalwart, too. Sometimes an insignificant element in a situation can hold an entire organization in check, and only a gentle approach can resolve the predicament.

The Judgment

The moment for action on a large scale has not yet arrived. The situation is not a hopeless or insoluble one: there is just one small element that stands in the way of resolution and ultimate success. Be satisfied with making preparations. Friendly persuasion is the answer rather than force or unduly rough argument. Although determination is important, it must be calmly and simply expressed.

The Image

The wind blows across the sky, buffeting the clouds, making them grow dense and heavy. The wind can only go so far, however – it does not possess the strength to turn the clouds to rain. When you are caught between an immovable object and an irresistible force, don't waste energy. Work in a subtle, gentle way – a drip of water wears away stone. Be determined but flexible, taking the line of least resistance but greatest persuasion.

The Lines

1 If you meet a situation that cannot be resolved, it might be judicious to make a tactical retreat and apply force from another, more original direction. Retreat is often the first step to victory.

2 Forcing an issue and laying yourself open to criticism and a brush-off will solve nothing. Be flexible, bide your time, and seek support from like-minded others.

3 At this moment the weak are strong, and anyone who attempts to press on relentlessly will be obstructed by time-wasting arguments. Success seems a long way off.

4 You may feel you are weak, but you will be capable of guiding the strongest person in the right direction. Do not be shy of offering advice. Truth overcomes error.

5 Be loyal to your beliefs. This may mean loyalty to a person, a group of friends or colleagues, or an idea, and may consist of simple enthusiasm or complete trust.

6 Success seems highly probable, but it will come through a combination of small circumstances. Be careful to consolidate, and don't push your luck.

ABOVE: **Sun**
gentleness, wind/wood, intuition

BELOW: **Ch'ien**
creativity, heaven, strength

---

10 LÜ ~ *Behavior*

ABOVE: **Ch'ien**
creativity, heaven, strength

BELOW: **Tui**
joy, lake, ecstasy

The hexagram focuses on behavior as general conduct rather than "manners." There is an emphasis on "class," which today is better expressed as consideration for those with whom we come into contact, whether rich or poor, fortunate or unfortunate. The weak can triumph by exercising good humor and natural wit.

The Judgment

In a situation when one person or organization is strong and the other weak, both can suffer: the weak can harry and worry the strong, while the strong can trample on the susceptibilities of the weak. Pleasant, decorous behavior can prove highly effective, even with difficult people – concentrate on cultivating good humor.

The Image

In life, it can sometimes be upsetting to realize that universal equality does not exist, and that some people are "higher" than others. It is important to remember that the person who seems to be "over" you is there by virtue, not by circumstance; do not be envious. In trying times, as long as inner worth and virtue corresponds with external rank and success, all is in order.

The Lines

1 Class, in the old sense of the word, is dead. Do not be impressed by anyone who seems to use birth as an excuse for appearing superior. Be comfortable with your own position.

2 Conviction and belief can result in isolation, especially if they are against current trends. Do not try to challenge anyone who disagrees; be firm and hold your ground.

3 Resist the temptation to overvalue yourself: know your weaknesses and don't get into danger by taxing your psychological or physical strength. Look before you leap.

4 You can be sure of success if you press forward steadily and without panic. Approach the danger ahead with caution; but even if your position seems weak, do not hesitate to hold firm.

5 Take off the rose-colored glasses and see things as they really are. In the cold light of day they may look dangerous. This is because they are. But be resolute.

6 It's over. If it has ended well, the result will be positive – though no one will know but yourself. Only when the dust has settled will you be able to see the real consequence.

11 T'AI ~ *Peace*

This is the most harmonious hexagram of all 64. Earth and heaven, flexibility and creativity, adaptability and strength are all working positively together. The Chinese associate this hexagram with spring, with its hopeful new beginnings, nature about to blossom, and animals preparing to breed.

The Judgment
There is a strong suggestion of the innocence and delight of the Garden of Eden, of absolute harmony and peace, universal positivity, problems resolved, and lasting pleasure and happiness. All are blessed: the good are in control, and the evil are routed. The meek have inherited the earth.

The Image
Good fortune and success abound, but do not neglect the situation. It is important to nurture peace and harmony, just as one waters and feeds a beautiful plant. Although everything is running smoothly and as it should, do not allow the situation to become wild and uncultivated – it could quickly become a confusing tangle of uncontrolled weeds. Any garden, no matter how perfect, needs a good, committed gardener, love and care, and continual vigilance.

The Lines
1 If you are in a position of power or influence, use it. Persuade others to join you, and work with them, not merely enjoying peace and plenty but spreading it abroad.

2 However irritated you may be by certain people, bear with them. They can be useful if they are properly approached and treated. Don't neglect any potential, even if it seems unpromising at first.

3 Even what seems perfect is subject to change: nothing stands still. And change can be for the worse, so be vigilant. A danger seen in time can be averted.

4 There are very few inherently evil people. Search for the positive, the good, and the useful in even the most unpromising material. Don't be superior – look for common ground.

5 It is when people work together that the most positive results are achieved. This applies most strongly when those people are extremely different from each other.

6 A warning: there will and must be change. Do not fight it. Hold your ground and don't be pushed around, but don't try to stop the tide from flowing.

ABOVE: **K'un**
flexibility, earth, adaptability

BELOW: **Ch'ien**
creativity, heaven, strength

12 P'I ~ *Stagnation*

ABOVE: **Ch'ien**
creativity, heaven, strength

BELOW: **K'un**
flexibility, earth, adaptability

Here, there is a great gap between heaven and earth. Without contact between them, there is nothing but a huge vacuum. Traditionally, this hexagram is connected with the natural decay of autumn, when growth has been completed but the harvest has not been gathered. Leaves fall, fruit rots on the trees, and early rain has beaten down the crops. But perhaps there may still be a chance to salvage the situation.

The Judgment
Bewilderment and agitation, weakness and cruelty, the inferior gaining ground and the superior under attack. Communication is difficult, and everything is out of order. Keep steadfast and true – hold on to your principles, and refuse to be subdued. If necessary, keep your peace and await your opportunity to gain ground.

The Image
You may receive an offer that seems impossible to refuse. Examine it well. The probability is that the gold and silver are merely lead, and that the shine will soon wear off. Developing your own resources requires no help from anyone, and can only make you stronger in the long run.

The Lines
1 You may have to retire from a position, or perhaps a battle, which you realize you cannot hold or win. Do so graciously and in good time, and you will avoid dishonor.

2 Accept any setbacks, and don't be tempted to try to overcome them by playing anyone else's game. A pause for thought is the best advice at the moment.

3 Those who have annoyed or dismayed you will soon realize the impossibility of their position. They will be deeply ashamed – even if they do not show it.

4 If you are called, answer the call. Take action and you will not fail – you cannot but impress those around you by an almost single-handed act.

5 The right man or woman has arrived. It may even be you. But any moment that demands action is a tricky one: keep your balance, prepare the ground carefully, and advance slowly.

6 Just as you may be called to action, you must know when to bring it to an end. But do not relax: continual vigilance will be needed to consolidate your success.

13 T'UNG JÊN ~ *Fraternity*

Flame flares upward toward heaven, the symbol of friendship and fraternity – brotherhood and sisterhood. The hexagram represents the peaceful companionship of equals. Among this group of equals, eventually one person is likely to become the leader. In times of peace, but also if necessary during more combative times, this person will be selflessly devoted to keeping everyone together in fellowship against the outside world.

The Judgment
The interests and opinions of the individual should be subjugated to those of humankind in general. The good leader, with clear aims and an inspiring vision, will insist, gently but firmly, on this – and under his or her strength and guidance even the most difficult task can be accomplished.

The Image
A fire needs to be watched, fed, tended, and carefully controlled – and so does any organization. Genuine fellowship needs a sense of order within it to be successful – a collection of people simply milling around without a clear aim or a focused purpose is useless, potentially chaotic, and will achieve nothing of worth.

The Lines
1 Things have started well, there has been no argument, and you have made no mistakes. Make sure that you have given your trust and opened your heart.

2 Keeping things to yourself can do no good: be frank and open, welcoming everyone's contribution to a problem or situation. Holding on to a problem will become stifling.

3 Suspicion raises its head; you may have reservations about your own or others' actions or intentions. Friendship and love begin to break up, and trust is weakened.

4 After any quarrel there is the possibility of reconciliation, however difficult and embarrassing. The situation will force you to renew trust and friendship, without which you cannot prosper.

5 Physical separation does not mean that you cannot be with a beloved in your heart. There will be grief, but real love must triumph; and when reunion comes it will be all the sweeter.

6 There is something fainthearted about your intentions, as if you mistrust friends and colleagues. Renew your trust; a long road lies ahead, but it finally reaches home.

ABOVE: **Ch'ien**
creativity, heaven, strength

BELOW: **Li**
fidelity, fire, vision

14 TA YU ~ *Belonging*

ABOVE: **Li**
fidelity, fire, vision

BELOW: **Ch'ien**
creativity, heaven, strength

The trigram Li, the flame that leaps up from the top of the hexagram, shows that the creativity of the subject is well illuminated and publicized, however weak the original action or thought may seem. The hexagram's meaning has been compared to Jesus' saying: "Blessed are the meek: for they shall inherit the earth." Modesty will gain strength through action.

The Judgment
Fortune shines on you and opportunity beckons. Great success awaits. Now is the time to fulfill your potential – use your inner strength to express your intention, put forward your theory, or whatever it is that you have always wanted to do. But express yourself with careful elegance and genuine modesty – do not spoil your good fortune by using clumsy force.

The Image
Fire in heaven may mean the power of the sun. The fiery planet stands for what "belongs," in a natural way, either to you or to the situation, as well as brightly illuminating the scene. The spotlight makes everything clear – both good and bad. Fight the bad, and promote the good.

The Lines
1 You haven't made any mistakes yet, but there are various barriers to be overcome. Guard against arrogance – look at the situation coolly, and don't waste your efforts.

2 You can take responsibility, and it may well soon be loaded upon you. Keep mobile and don't stick in the mud. In important matters, be sure to accept help when it is offered.

3 Be generous and magnanimous, and put your worldly possessions at the disposal of any friend who needs help. You will not lose by this action.

4 If you find yourself among people who seem more powerful or better placed than yourself, avoid jealousy or envy. This way, you will remain free to act as you think best.

5 A favorable situation. The people around you are sincere and genuine. However, don't allow the situation to become too relaxed. The natural conclusion is insolence, so remain dignified at all times.

6 Keep your balance, however powerful you become, and remain modest. If you stand on your dignity you may well find your feet on muddy ground or shifting sands.

15 CH'IEN ~ *Modesty*

This hexagram represents modesty – the uncommon power often possessed by those people who give the impression of being "ordinary" or even powerless, but who by simplicity of character are able to shape events and influence people to a previously unexpected extent. In the end, the respect and admiration they command results in their exaltation to a position of honor.

The Judgment

The balance of nature – an ending turning toward a beginning, a beginning inevitably reaching an end – also affects humankind. But knowledge of your own character and power enables you to control and shape events to some extent. There is no need to boast of your achievements – it is sufficient that modesty is its own reward.

The Image

Fight against extremism either in behavior or in ambition: both the mountaintops and the bottom of an abyss are formidably forbidding. Being moderate, and keeping to the middle ground is safer, and not necessarily dull or unadventurous. Equalizing extremes creates just and equable positions where everyone can thrive.

The Lines

1 Simplicity should be the keynote. Free your mind of clutter and complete tasks quickly. Be modest in the demands you make on others, but also on yourself, in order to avoid disappointment or frustration.

2 The way that you express modesty is important here. When other people are convinced that you are truly modest, you will be trusted and have a natural authority.

3 Great achievements make you well-known and admired. If you allow your achievements to dazzle yourself, however, admiration will soon turn to scorn.

4 Remember that even modesty should not be overdone. If someone in authority confides in you, keep the confidence, and do not be tempted by pride to use it against others.

5 If you need to rebuke someone, be rational and as inoffensive as possible. The appearance of superiority invariably leads to dislike and a refusal to be helpful.

6 Don't blame anyone else for your own mistakes, and be prepared to excuse other people for theirs. Remember to be as critical of yourself as you are of others.

ABOVE: **K'un**
flexibility, earth, adaptability

BELOW: **Kên**
obduracy, mountain, rest

16 YÜ ~ *Eagerness*

Whatever you do at this moment is likely to be greeted with enthusiasm and eagerly carried forward. The hexagram represents one of the essential laws of nature and human existence – that things, left to themselves, follow the line of least resistance. The upper trigram is forceful, while the lower is adaptable and flexible, representing obedience to what seems to be inevitable.

The Judgment

You find yourself a leader, for others believe in you and sympathize with your objectives. But harmony is paramount. Take the wishes of others into account – you cannot make any progress whatsoever against the general view. Your energy and enthusiasm will enable you to delegate successfully, and you will be supported by willing helpers.

The Image

As thunder lightens and dispels a heavy atmosphere, so pleasure relieves tension, bringing relief. Now is the time to do whatever you enjoy in life and lifts your heart. The hexagram is especially connected to music and dance – and the part they play in comforting, relaxing, and enthusing those who respond.

The Lines

1 Forget self – this is not a time for boasting about your aims or achievements, or for relying on influential friends or relatives. Any show of pride or pomposity will inevitably result in disaster.

2 Others may be misled by the promise of success. You see things much more clearly and may have to spend time explaining reality to those with a less realistic vision.

3 Seize the right moment in which to act; hesitation will be fatal. If you are uncertain, look to the man or woman most likely to give good advice on the situation.

4 Someone is absolutely certain about the action that should be taken. Is it you or someone else? In any case, his, her, or your advice will have complete integrity.

5 There is considerable tension, which may seem so great that you find it impossible to act. But it has a purpose: it prevents sudden, overenthusiastic, and rash action.

6 Your enthusiasm may well be dampened by events, but this will probably mean that reality has at last made itself felt, and has punctured the balloon of overoptimism.

ABOVE: **Chên**
exhilaration, thunder, provocation

BELOW: **K'un**
flexibility, earth, adaptability

17 SUI ~ Complaisance

The hexagram is said to represent an older man bowing to a young girl, therefore giving her a sense of her worth. By respecting the opinions of other people, even those whom you consider less experienced and informed than yourself, you can gain support and loyalty that will serve you well when you or your actions need it most.

The Judgment
Be as adaptable as you can in your situation, and remember that promotion comes only after a period of serving in the ranks. Suddenly assuming authority over others without demonstrating that you understand them and their problems is not calculated to gain you either respect or obedience, and is more likely to result in the opposite. Be consistent and true in your actions, and follow your conscience at all times.

The Image
Relax into your problems rather than worrying continually about them. Time taken for leisure and rest is time most usefully employed and enjoyed. Be comfortable in the surroundings in which you find yourself – go with the flow rather than draining your energies by useless struggle and resistance.

The Lines
1 A leader must be open to constructive criticism and take account of it, but without being dissuaded from any action that clearly seems right and proper.

2 A mixture of acquaintances – reliable and unreliable, good and bad – may seem attractive; but in the end, time given to undeserving people is always time wasted.

3 Your reluctance to drop old friends is admirable, however unworthy they may have proved; but finally it is the best course. Misdirected loyalty can be a wasteful and damaging emotion.

4 Few people are immune to flattery, and it is harmless so long as it is recognized for what it is. But do not rely on sycophants. Learn to recognize them instead.

5 Everyone needs a goal, whether it is pleasure, power, honesty, or even crime. The choice, or the decision to change, is one of the most important in life.

6 In most people's lives, a "father-figure" or "mother-figure" emerges. This person is seen as our "leader." Choose well, and remember that even great men and women are human.

ABOVE: **Tui**
joy, lake, ecstasy

BELOW: **Chên**
exhilaration, thunder, provocation

18 KU ~ Disintegration

ABOVE: **Kên**
obduracy, mountain, rest

BELOW: **Sun**
gentleness, wind/wood, intuition

The Chinese hexagram represents a bowl in which worms are breeding, indicating decay. The fight between the trigrams K'en and Sun has reached a state of stalemate, and there are strong feelings of guilt on both sides. But peace talks must be held and a solution found that will not damage either side too greatly. The meaning of the hexagram is not merely that the situation is harmful, but that a way must be found to repair it.

The Judgment
Human fallibility contributed to the situation, and human ingenuity must repair it. Do not shrink from confronting a difficult problem, but seize and subdue it to common sense leavened with goodwill. Make proper preparations, and once you have embarked on a course of action review the situation carefully. To allow the ending to progress to a new beginning, the state of stagnation must give way to action.

The Image
Indignation must be brought to bear and properly directed. When it has had the effect of persuading people to action, it must be calmed and a firm and lasting solution found, which will satisfy everyone.

The Lines
1 Inflexibility is the main problem here. It should not be too difficult to find ways of relaxing it so that the necessary reorganization can take place.

2 Leaping in with both feet is not a good idea. Tread carefully; be tactful but firm, so that mistakes can be corrected without giving too much offense to the guilty.

3 The bull may wreck the china shop, but perhaps the china was imperfect. Overenthusiasm can be effective, but gentleness will avoid damage to relationships.

4 If you continue to take no action, things will go from bad to worse. The present course of events has its roots in the past. If it continues, embarrassment is inevitable.

5 Past neglect results in present impasse. With the help of others, many wrongs can be put right. If it is impossible to correct the situation completely, a small improvement is always better than nothing.

6 There are times when a little introversion is not a bad thing. Self-improvement might require the neglect of others' problems in order to set your own life on the right course.

19 LIN ~ *Command*

The meaning of this hexagram is complex, referring to the relationship between a leader and those who are led, a certain pride that is necessary to those who lead, and the attitude taken by a leader to the necessary work of leadership and the impulse to action. The hexagram's ancient meaning has been translated as "becoming great" – perhaps suggesting the inherent problems of authority.

The Judgment
Spring is here – a time of joy, hope, progress, and rebirth. Success awaits, but you must concentrate all your personal resources on making the best of this precious time. Spring must inevitably give way to summer, fall, winter – and while enjoying this most delightful of seasons, it is necessary to make adequate preparations for the more problematic times ahead.

The Image
The wise leader is always as conscious of his or her knowledge as of the power this gives, and must also be conscious of the needs of those who can profit from it. The experience of a single person, relayed to others, can be precious, illuminating a whole generation, and excluding no one.

The Lines
1 Fashion is a dangerous thing. It may be fun to follow, but it must be resisted if it leads in the wrong direction. Rely on your instinct: speak out if the fashion is misdirected.

2 The ups and downs of life may be infuriating and even damaging, but they are inevitable. Learn from both, so that neither throws you off course.

3 Keep a clear eye on life, even when you are at your most relaxed. Don't let others mistake an easygoing good nature for weakness. If mistaken, don't conceal the mistake: correct it.

4 Look for ability in every direction. Do not assume that because a person is different to you, he or she is wrong or incapable. Learn to recognize "difference" as a possible talent.

5 Once you trust a friend or colleague, make that trust complete. Recognize the expertise of others and give them the freedom to exercise it.

6 It is probably a mistake to withdraw completely from any situation. Even if self-interest does not require it, a return to a neglected aspect of life can benefit others.

ABOVE: **K'un**
flexibility, earth, adaptability

BELOW: **Tui**
joy, lake, ecstasy

20 KUAN ~ *Looking On*

ABOVE: **Sun**
gentleness, wind/wood, intuition

BELOW: **K'un**
flexibility, earth, adaptability

The shape of the hexagram resembles a tower in ancient China. As well as offering a broad view of the country, the tower could also be seen for miles around as a landmark. Consequently, Kuan has two meanings: observing others, and being observed – thinking consciously about others' actions and reactions, and offering them an example that they might care to follow. Here, there is the sense of understanding your own life, and offering it as an example to other people.

The Judgment
A good example can be a powerful influence, and may even have the effect of changing someone's life. It is always important to keep your own image in mind. And "image" does not only mean the outward appearance, but also the inward reality – not how you appear to behave, but how you really act.

The Image
If you are moral and determined to do right, you are unlikely to be deceived by anyone who is immoral and liable to act wrongly. The latter is indeed likely to be swayed by your excellent example. However, if you are not firmly in the right, you may find yourself being tempted to behave badly.

The Lines
1 Does it seem as if nobody understands you? It is possible but you will still have an affect on others. Before offering advice to other people, try to put yourself in their place and understand their reactions.

2 Watching others and analyzing their behavior might be entertaining, but merely observing will not get you very far. It is action that is needed.

3 Know yourself by all means, but do not merely use self-knowledge to forward your own affairs. Think about the effect you and your actions may have on other people.

4 When dealing with others, think of yourself as a guest in their life. A guest is not impertinent and does not interfere, but merely gently advises if and when asked.

5 Always be ready to examine your own motives, but don't brood about them. Think how they affect others. Good results bring inner satisfaction.

6 Try to stand outside life: look at your life objectively, as you would observe that of an alien creature from outer space. This should enable you to see your motives more clearly.

21 SHIH HO ~ *Clenched Teeth*

The hexagram represents an open mouth, with the teeth clenched on an obstacle. To close your mouth, you must bite through the impediment. Similarly, when criminal activity goes on, the "law" must be used to resolve the situation. Here, the "law" might be the formal law, or your own private sense of what is right. Both should be vigorously used when necessary.

The Judgment
Perhaps someone appears to be getting in your way, obstructing your actions by their personal, selfish motives. A confrontation of some sort is the only way forward – the obstruction will not vanish of its own accord. Keep a balance, however, being neither so forceful and violent as to do permanent damage, or so gentle and understanding as to have no effect. The best results will be reached by being firm but fair.

The Image
A sense of justice is important here – work from a clear sense of fitting the punishment to the crime, and administer that punishment quickly and cleanly. Remember that punishment should not be for its own sake, but in order to correct and reform.

The Lines
1 Be gentle when punishing a first offense. Issue a warning. If the rebuke is ignored, that is the time to be firmer, gradually increasing the punishment until it has its desired effect.

2 It is easy to go too far, and in sudden anger to punish so severely that recovery is impossible. Always try to keep anger at bay, and learn to think before responding.

3 Punishment is only truly effective when it is administered by the right person. It may be best to delegate. If you must punish, be prepared to be disliked for it.

4 Great strength of personality will be needed to overcome the most obstructive opposition. Recognize the difficulties, make a firm effort, and you will succeed.

5 The Chinese text advises us to be pure as gold and as strong as its color, yellow, which is associated with purity and impartiality. If you recognize your responsibilities you should avoid mistakes.

6 Here is a man or woman so obdurate that punishment is inevitable. Unfortunately, the punishment may have little effect, for he or she is deaf to all argument.

ABOVE: **Li**
fidelity, fire, vision

BELOW: **Chên**
exhilaration, thunder, provocation

22 PI ~ *Symmetry*

ABOVE: **Kên**
obduracy, mountain, rest

BELOW: **Li**
fidelity, fire, vision

Symmetry – a restful stillness and conscious balance – is necessary for any partnership if it is to be steady yet malleable, orderly yet flexible, able to bend when stricken by rough winds, capable of great strength when tested, and not be prone to disintegrate into muddle and disorderly weakness. The hexagram represents fire rising to illuminate the craggiest rocks of the mountain.

The Judgment
Beauty may bring great rewards, but it is only an outward phenomenon. It should be very carefully used if in the end there is not to be disappointment. Beauty can provoke desire and envy. These emotions should be stilled, then inward and outward beauty can be seen for what they are – giving great pleasure, but only offering the most obvious rewards.

The Image
The fire may illuminate the mountain, but it does not make it easier to climb. Although beauty delights and attracts us, it can have no effect on the important matters of life – it poses questions rather than answering them, comments only in a flippant way upon character, and should be ignored when important matters are to be discussed.

The Lines
1 If you were offered a lift in a car driven by a drunken friend, you might think it best to walk. Consider the alternatives and choose carefully, paying the utmost attention to your own safety and dignity.

2 No matter what you wear, all you are doing is ornamenting your body. Your real self, the most important part of you, is still concealed. Avoid vanity.

3 You may feel comfortable, contented, and happy. Don't sink into lethargy, though – continual watchfulness is the price of comfort and happiness, and will preserve them.

4 The partner whose approaches you are considering may seem unworthy, but maybe you are simply being snobbish and are missing the chance of a worthwhile relationship.

5 It is nonsense to think that you have little or nothing to offer, and that no one would be interested in your ideas. Offer your assistance sincerely – it will be welcomed.

6 You are naked to the world. Your true worth is clearly seen for what it is, unclothed and uncluttered by disguise or unnecessary ornament. Simplicity has its own rewards.

23 PO ~ *Breaking Up*

Here, the power of yin – the female part of a personality – pushes upward and undermines the masculine power of yang. Indeed, yin is so powerful at this time that it threatens to overcome yang completely. Consequently, this is not a situation without danger – if it continues, something has simply got to give. The top line of the hexagram represents a roof – the rising energy shatters the roof and the house collapses.

The Judgment

The sense of deterioration is such that there is not much to be said for fighting against prevailing circumstances. It can appear to be a depressing time, with superior minds being overcome by inferior minds, and the mediocre overwhelming the elite. Be still and quiet, and ignore any suggestions that submission is equal to cowardice. Avoid taking action – do not feel under pressure to make things happen.

The Image

The respect and support of those around you will consolidate your position. If you are generous, understanding, and helpful, your position will be as firm as that of a mountain resting on the earth.

The Lines

1 Someone may be trying to undermine your position, perhaps by lying – or at least being economical with the truth – to your friends and colleagues. At the moment, you can do nothing but wait on events.

2 You seem to be standing alone while your position grows weaker and weaker. Be very watchful indeed. Take no rash action, and above all bend to the wind.

3 There is one person on whom you can depend – probably someone very close to you. Seek out him or her, and be trustful. You will upset your enemies, but who cares?

4 At last, the forces of opposition are about to crumble. Even your enemies will submit to your will, and bitterly regret their previous actions. All will go well.

5 Happy days are here again. Your enemies are now the unfortunate ones: ill-nature eventually destroys itself.

6 Now is the time to reap what you have sown. The good and the positive will be rewarded, finding fulfillment in their influence and effectiveness, while the world of the ill-inclined and the negative will crash down.

ABOVE: **Kên**
obduracy, mountain, rest

BELOW: **K'un**
flexibility, earth, adaptability

24 FU ~ *The Pivot*

ABOVE: **K'un**
flexibility, earth, adaptability

BELOW: **Chên**
exhilaration, thunder, provocation

The hexagram is associated with the winter solstice, and thus with the turning point of the year. The dark days of winter have passed, and the light begins to increase – this is the pivotal moment when difficulty and danger drops away and easier and less fatiguing times are ahead.

The Judgment

The cyclical movement of nature takes its inexorable course – the old order changes, yielding to the new. There is no need to interfere in this process, because everything is working perfectly already – after a time of disintegration, order and growth will return. It is a time for reaching out to others with similar ideas, and bonding for the general good. Selfishness should be rejected – it is a time for working together.

The Image

Take it easy for a while – find some time to relax and replenish your energies. Take stock and consider your position; rest and consider events, meditating on the past and the present, preparing yourself for the future. Above all, do not think that every problem can be quickly solved, and guard against leaping in where angels would fear to tread.

The Lines

1 Sudden conversions are difficult: clear your mind of past error. It may not be possible to reverse every bad or mistaken decision. Do your best to mitigate any ill effects.

2 If you feel alone and devoid of strength, follow the best example of people with whom you can identify, and model yourself on the person you admire the most.

3 Avoid vacillation – abruptly reversing every decision because you doubt its probity simply makes muddle worse. Be moderate, and think before you act.

4 Deciding to do the right thing for the right reason almost always brings its own reward, even if some sort of payoff is the last thing you have in mind.

5 This is confession time: do not take refuge in excuses – confess your fault and apologize for it immediately. No one will think any the worse of you – on the contrary, you will win respect for your honesty.

6 Doing the right thing is good, doing it at the right time is even better. If you put off a decision, perhaps through stubbornness, the result will be catastrophe.

25 WU WANG ~ *Simplicity*

True innocence results in natural goodness. The moment you begin to calculate the result of your attitudes and actions, you have lost your innocence, and self-consciousness and awkwardness will take its place. Your plans will then be made for ulterior profit and personal gratification rather than for the benefit of everyone. The unforeseen may play a leading part in distracting you from the right and true path.

The Judgment
Natural goodness is more common than natural evil, and following the innermost heart almost always results in noble conduct. Following an impulse that is pure will invariably result in success; but this should not be mistaken for being selfish, and doing whatever you choose in an unthinking way. Be calm, moderate, and reflective – do not drain your resources by trying to analyze every likely permutation of your actions.

The Image
The truly good person possesses the innocence and natural creativity of a child – looking for the good in everyone and everything, and eager to encourage it whenever the right moment offers itself.

The Lines
1 A thought that springs straight from the heart is always good; do not hesitate to follow it and carry it through. Happiness will inevitably follow.

2 In the Biblical phrase, whatever you turn your hand to, do it with all your might – for its own sake and not thinking of the result. Anything that you take on will then succeed.

3 We can suffer good or ill apparently at random, often as the result of someone else's good or ill fortune. Accept this without anguish, taking the fortune of the time.

4 You are the most powerful part of your life, so be true to yourself. Nothing that really belongs to you can then be lost. If you allow your judgment to be swayed by the wrong people, injury will certainly follow.

5 If you suffer accidental damage through no fault of your own, accept it quietly. No permanent damage will be done, and no great loss will be suffered.

6 Wait for the right moment before acting. Progress will not be made by premature action. Bulldozing thoughtlessly ahead is not the way to success.

ABOVE: **Ch'ien**
creativity, heaven, strength

BELOW: **Chên**
exhilaration, thunder, provocation

26 TA CH'U ~ *Small is Good*

ABOVE: **Kên**
obduracy, mountain, rest

BELOW: **Ch'ien**
creativity, heaven, strength

Stillness, of mind or of body, can represent real strength and power. In stillness, you may collect your thoughts, restrain rash action, and build up strength of mind and body. This is extremely important when a situation requires steely determination and, if all else fails, forthright action in the face of determined opposition.

The Judgment
Quiet, inner strength corresponds with great firmness of mind. During quiet times, good orderly habits keep things in harmony. But when the energy has shifted, it requires a strong personality to remain undistracted. If you remain strong and focused, your natural power will be affirmed and renewed, and the most important actions can be performed with assurance and grace.

The Image
The past is not simply history – once it was the present and was as important to you as today. Life brings experience, and the understanding of that experience, carefully considered and remembered, is important at times of stress. It can be applied to the present and indeed to the future, making your decisions well-founded and wise.

The Lines
1 Faced with an apparently immovable object, do not attempt to break through. Stop and think. A way around will eventually present itself.

2 Pause. Wait. Do not expend energy unnecessarily. If the car breaks down, do not tinker ignorantly with the engine. Save your energy. Help will arrive.

3 The path seems clear, but beware – there may be hidden dangers ahead. Advance cautiously, keeping your eye firmly on your goal, and mustering your skills and resources to deal with any obstacles.

4 Plan ahead for when danger might approach. Don't panic – think of the possible consequences and forestall them by carefully considered action.

5 This line reinforces line four, above: if the nature of a danger is thoroughly understood, it can be disarmed much more easily than if opposition is random and ill-planned.

6 At last the logjam has broken and consequently the situation is much happier. This is no doubt the result of your own resolute and disinterested action.

27 I ~ *Sustenance*

The hexagram resembles a mouth – the top and bottom yang lines represent the lips, and the yin lines between them indicate that the mouth is open. We take in physical nourishment through our mouths, but we need mental sustenance, too. The hexagram represents nourishment both of the body and the mind – the need to keep yourself in good physical condition, but also mentally alert and emotionally stable – the one often more dependent upon the other than we may suspect. Physical and mental exercise are emphasized, and the value of both.

The Judgment
We provide sustenance for ourselves, but also for others; and the way in which we "feed" others (either emotionally or physically) says much about us – whether we are truly caring, or looking after our own interests by only caring for those whose help we need.

The Image
Mental and emotional sustenance are vital to the health of the individual, and should contribute to general serenity. Like the physical diet, they rely on balance, quality, and the correct quantity, but of thought rather than food.

The Lines
1 It may be that you envy those who are better off than you, and who are able to live independently and without relying on others. Do not give in to these feelings – jealousy is the most sterile and wasteful of emotions.

2 If you have to rely on other people, it is difficult to avoid feeling patronized. But if you are making as much effort as possible, accept any offers of help graciously – it can later be paid back in full.

3 The word "sustenance" does not include what has become important from sheer desire or lust. The pursuit of pleasure as though it is all-important leads only to disaster.

4 Working for the good of others, it is best to seek help – you alone cannot achieve as much as if you lead a like-minded team.

5 If you feel that you are not achieving as much as you would like, do not be afraid of seeking advice from someone you admire, and whose assistance will help you to success.

6 Confidence in your own power and satisfaction in past achievements leads to the assurance that you can undertake any task, with a good chance of success.

ABOVE: **Kên**
obduracy, mountain, rest

BELOW: **Chên**
exhilaration, thunder, provocation

28 TA KUO ~ *Power to the Strong*

The very shape of the hexagram is a warning: the yang lines show that there is strength within, but the top and bottom lines are yin – the outside is broken. The Chinese image of the hexagram is of a strong beam with weak ends, which is liable to collapse. The situation cannot be allowed to continue, for everything is out of balance – the strong are not protected; the appearance of weakness can encourage attack from outside, and that attack may be successful.

The Judgment
Is the load too heavy for you to bear? Do you feel as if you are approaching "breaking point"? The situation is only temporary, but it is nevertheless vital to protect yourself sufficiently against attack. Action is required, but this should be measured and thoughtful, not forceful or violent. Build up your defenses deliberately, and take particular care at a time of change.

The Image
The lower trigram, Sun, represents a tree standing firm in shaking ground, while the upper trigram, Tui, represents joy – retain your positive and optimistic attitude, because the signs are that you will win in the end.

The Lines
1 Caution is the watchword – even exaggerated caution, for the time being. Remember that a distinctive plan cannot succeed unless it is carefully organized.

2 The situation is certainly unusual; you will do well to go along with the majority for now, keeping your own individual plans on the back burner.

3 If you are striding ahead, regardless of the opinion of others, you cannot expect their support when you need it most. Carefully examine the consequences before throwing yourself into action.

4 Work with others, at least for the present time; do not use the situation for personal power and profit. You can become a leader, but only with the support of others.

5 If you only collaborate with those who are of your own mind, you may lose your sense of balance. Take in all opinions, and carefully consider the options.

6 Is a sacrifice being asked of you? It may be one that in all conscience you cannot avoid. Be courageous, and stick to your principles. Events will reach their natural conclusion.

ABOVE: **Tui**
joy, lake, ecstasy

BELOW: **Sun**
gentleness, wood/wind, intuition

29 K'AN ~ *Water*

This is the hexagram that, above all others, suggests imminent danger – not necessarily physical or financial, but psychological – perhaps arising out of foolishness or premature action. If you behave correctly, you should escape; but you must not ignore the situation. Acquaint yourself thoroughly with the hazards ahead, face them, understand them, and finally, and most importantly, deal with them.

The Judgment
Danger, like pain, is a warning: properly understood, it can be used as a means of protection; for when we are aware of it we can build up our defenses. It is important not to glamorize the situation, but to look for its reality, no matter how harsh.

The Image
Water does not hesitate when faced with a dangerous channel or a perilous cliff: it looks for the easiest and most direct way over and through it. Water also flows on without pause. Be thorough and resolute in your actions. Having decided on your course, pursue it relentlessly. Always be true to your essential nature, no matter what the prevailing conditions around you.

The Lines
1 Do not make friends with danger. Treat it with respect, by all means; but if you allow it to become a way of life, you will grow careless and lose your way.

2 Do not imagine that with just one leap you can be free of danger. First, make sure the abyss does not overwhelm you – then weigh up the situation calmly and carefully before making your move.

3 For the moment, dig a shelter and stay there. Every single step you make is fraught with danger, so be still and patient – do not move until you see a bit of light.

4 Do not even attempt to talk your way out of difficulty. Now is not the time for equivocation. Nothing other than complete honesty and frankness will do.

5 Do not be overly ambitious or imagine that you can get out of the present trouble at once, and take several steps forward on the way. For now, be content with safety.

6 You have lost your way, and find yourself shackled by your circumstances. The danger is at its most extreme. Any action is liable to make things worse. Make no move.

ABOVE: **K'an**
the abyss, water, danger

BELOW: **K'an**
the abyss, water, danger

30 LI ~ *Cherishing*

ABOVE: **Li**
faithfulness, fire, vision

BELOW: **Li**
faithfulness, fire, vision

The hexagram represents the desire for the good, and the instinct to cling to the best: perhaps to your dearest ambitions, closest companions, and best-loved friends. The Chinese compare it to a flame that feeds upon its fuel – the material which keeps it alight and shining. Without its fuel it would be starved of what keeps it alive.

The Judgment
Left unattended, fire will burn quickly and fiercely before extinguishing itself, leaving nothing but a pile of ashes. Fire needs careful tending and nourishment – and the better the quality of the fuel, the brighter and more constant the flame. Every light is kept shining by some force or energy; and humankind equally needs to cling to what most strongly motivates and sustains it.

The Image
The double Li trigrams that make up the Li hexagram represent the sun's course through the day – shining and spreading its light into every corner of the world and upon every human being. We must learn to see ourselves and our motives with all the clarity of the brightest sunlight shining into the deepest, most shadowy crevice.

The Lines
1 In the early morning you wake from sleep and begin to think and act; still half-asleep, you may act carelessly and prematurely. Thoughtful deliberation is needed.

2 The Chinese see the midday sun as bright yellow – the color of purity of thought and action. Do not allow yourself to be distracted from the proper course.

3 The sun rises and sets. Every day – and every life – must end. Prepare yourself for endings and face them with the courage and conviction that you have done well.

4 Fire consumes what it feeds on; the best fuel lasts longest. Learn to pace yourself, restrain hysteria and excitability, and move through life with a measured tread.

5 Complete success is a turning point, but perhaps your triumph and the achievement of your aims has resulted in overbearing vanity. Disillusion and sorrow will surely follow. Where do you go from here?

6 Self-criticism is excellent, but not when taken to extremes. We are all human. Small errors can be excused, but serious personal faults must be rooted out immediately.

31 HSIEN ~ *Courtship*

Hsien is the hexagram most strongly associated with the attraction – sexual and emotional – felt by one human being for another, whether between man and woman or between members of the same sex. It relates to romance, permanent partnership, and possibly marriage – to the basic emotional relationships that lie at the heart of any social group.

The Judgment
Do not let yourself be entirely carried away by emotion. Think of the difference between courtship and seduction – the one involving real love, care, and nurturing, the other composed of mere sexual attraction and selfishness. Real love implies courtship, persuasion, and an equality that cements a permanent emotional bond.

The Image
Be flexible, and keep your mind open to new ideas. Listen to others even if you eventually disagree with their judgment. If you turn a blind eye and ear to all advice, other people will eventually cease to attempt to counsel you. Although this may be peaceful and agreeable for a while, it may also deprive you of real friends and support.

The Lines
1 The beginning of wisdom is often almost imperceptible. Remember that a first instinct means nothing unless you allow it full play, think about it, and nurture it.

2 When you have tested your instinct to the full, and only then, act upon it. Remember that to neglect an intuition means that you are denying full expression to your most intimate emotions.

3 Is your inhibition the result of indecision? It is wise not to pursue every instinct at a gallop, but beware that your hesitation does not result in an opportunity being lost.

4 Listen to the inner voice of your heart. You know from past experience whether this can be trusted. Sometimes, rarely, you must disobey it. But at least listen to it.

5 Emotions spring from your deep unconscious self. When emotions are genuine, it is almost impossible to disobey them without causing psychological damage.

6 Idle talk will do no good at all. Think before you speak – not only about the truth of your words, but about the effect they will have on other people.

ABOVE: **Tui**
joy, lake, ecstasy

BELOW: **Kên**
obduracy, mountain, rest

32 HÊNG ~ *Permanence*

ABOVE: **Chên**
exhilaration, thunder, provocation

BELOW: **Sun**
gentleness, wood/wind, intuition

This hexagram concentrates on permanent relationships – not, as does Hsien, above, on the emotional or sexual attraction which draws two people together, but on the qualities in them which link them permanently. It reflects those elements in two people's personalities that complement each other and make two different individuals act as one consistent entity.

The Judgment
Why are you here, what are you doing, where are you going? "The meaning of life" is a question to which everyone must find an answer, even if the answer is that there is no answer. Two individuals with strong, contrasting feelings about the purpose of their lives will find it extremely difficult to bind themselves together in a relationship.

The Image
Although the exhilaration of a thunderstorm and the tranquillity of a gentle wind seem poles apart, both are a part of nature. Mankind partakes of the nature of both and must learn to understand how to comprehend them harmoniously, without being either too much the voice of thunder or too consistently the murmur of a breeze.

The Lines
1 If you demand too much of yourself, or indeed of others, you will be disappointed unless you take all the time you need in which to accomplish it. Haste will have a negative result.

2 Are you aiming too high? Attempting to lift too great a weight? Sheer determination can and will achieve much, but control your ambition if you truly mean to succeed.

3 You may feel humiliated; consider whether you have not perhaps brought this upon yourself by yielding to depression or guilt, or by capricious behavior.

4 The man who asked the way was told, "You should not be starting from here." Do not search for a lost needle in a dark room. Make sure conditions are right before acting.

5 However much you respect, admire, and love someone else, do not persistently react and respond to their views and opinions. Be adaptable – but form your own opinions.

6 Violent running on the spot may improve your health, but does not actually lead anywhere. Avoid enormous effort that is merely exercised for its own sake.

33 TUN ~ *Passive Resistance*

When faced with overwhelming opposition or what seem to be insuperable difficulties, do not waste precious time and energy by engaging in overt battle. Instead, sit back, take a deep breath, and consider what can be achieved by passive resistance. If, when losing the tug-of-war, you let go of the rope, the opposing team will fall over. There is then enormous advantage to be taken.

The Judgment

Fall back in the face of a powerful enemy. But plan your withdrawal – you are not running away in a panic, you are always preparing to continue the fight. When you can, dig ditches and lay mines to stop the enemy's advance; and watch for the moment when you can pause, gather your strength, and put a new plan into effect.

The Image

When someone plans to take advantage of you, do not waste time in irrelevant anger or, even worse, jealousy. Preoccupation with your competitor or enemy will blind you to ways of advancing your own cause. Calmly think of the general picture, consider your strategy carefully, then bring your opponent to a standstill.

The Lines

1 When retreating it is important not to engage with the enemy: you are for the moment the weaker of the two. Keep out of the way, escaping immediate danger.

2 It may be difficult, but consider why at present your opponent has the advantage. It may be that he or she is in the right. Does that mean that you are in the wrong?

3 If you are trying to get out of a difficult situation but are trapped by circumstance, turn this to your advantage by yielding on small points, reserving your right to oppose on greater ones.

4 Avoid bitterness – and importantly, do not show any rancor. Your support is important: depriving your opponent of it will weaken him or her, perhaps fatally.

5 There is a right time for retreat, just as there is a right time for advance. Seize the moment, and be firm: do not be put off by suggestions that tomorrow will be better.

6 The situation is perfectly clear. There is no point in delay. You are free to go. Once you have realized this, depression will lift, and you will feel light-hearted and at ease.

ABOVE: **Ch'ien**
creativity, heaven, strength

BELOW: **Kên**
obduracy, mountain, rest

34 TA CHUANG ~ *The Immovable*

ABOVE: **Chên**
exhilaration, thunder, provocation

BELOW: **Ch'ien**
creativity, heaven, strength

This is a very powerful hexagram, the three solid yang lines at the bottom supporting the lightness of the upper trigram. Creativity and strength thunder forth and can conquer almost any situation. The inner power of your personality overcomes any obstacles in your path, while the outer image impresses those who might otherwise doubt your strength and potency.

The Judgment

The consciousness of your own strength and power is so considerable that you may be tempted to think yourself always and inevitably right – and you may act prematurely for the same reason. Remember to think every situation through, and ask yourself every conceivable question about your attitude to it, before acting.

The Image

Underlining the Judgment, the Image asks you to make quite sure that justice is on your side, to ensure that you take no action which interferes with natural justice. At the moment your power is so great that it could, if exercised wrongly, lead to great injury – not only to your own affairs but to those of others, including your family.

The Lines

1 If you are in an insubordinate position but suddenly find yourself in a position of power, be especially careful before using it – rash behavior could lead to a calamity.

2 Barriers crumble. But in rushing to jump them before they are finally down and the dust has settled, you may fall and find yourself in the midst of that rubble.

3 However carefully you proceed, you could become entangled in a web of complex problems. The utmost care and the most thorough preparation are essential.

4 Tranquil persistence is the best way forward. The less you show your muscle, the more smoothly you will progress and the less overt opposition you will arouse.

5 Everything seems perfectly simple. All opposition appears to have crumbled. The way ahead seems clear. And all this is as it should be – at the moment, only a fool would make a mistake.

6 Have you gone too far? Has easy progress lulled you into a sense of false security? If so, pause, consider the situation, and go forward with greater care.

35 CHIN ~ *Breakthrough*

This is a time of breakthrough, when new light is thrown not only on your current problems but perhaps also on your entire lifestyle. The image of the sun rising at dawn suggests a new start, progress, enlightenment, expansion, and a completely fresh vision of what life could mean for you and those nearest to you.

The Judgment

Perhaps you are in a commanding position, and are supported by others who may be weaker but have greater insight than you. Or maybe you are able to offer support and assistance to those in a stronger position, and they are able to rise as the result of your aid and take you with them. Progress can be gained in either of these two ways.

The Image

Before your actions can be seen as entirely disinterested and springing from purely altruistic motives, you must make sure that this is indeed the situation. Examine yourself and your inner motivations with complete honesty, and make every effort to ensure that you are neither taking undue advantage of anyone else's hard work, nor of anyone else's original ideas.

The Lines

1 You are unsure whether your ideas or opinion are acceptable to the person to whom you must put them. Determine to press ahead, even if there is opposition.

2 You cannot get through to the person to whom you need to put your ideas or your opinions. If you cannot make progress now, wait until the right moment arrives.

3 If you need the help of other people to put your ideas into operation, do not hesitate to ask. It is better to progress with others' help than have a standstill that may be lasting.

4 No doubt you can make a considerable profit by pressing ahead with a dubious enterprise. But you will be found out, and the result will be calamitous.

5 Modesty is always a virtue, and particularly so when you are triumphant. But gain and loss are equally immaterial in the greater scheme of things. What matters is the use you make of them.

6 Go on the offensive only if you are sure that a certain amount of force is necessary. It can be dangerous, especially if you attack those with whom you are unfamiliar.

ABOVE: **Li**
fidelity, fire, vision

BELOW: **K'un**
flexibility, earth, adaptability

36 MING I ~ *Sunset*

ABOVE: **K'un**
flexibility, earth, adaptability

BELOW: **Li**
fidelity, fire, vision

The sun has set – the situation is dark and will remain so for some time. The Chinese text speaks of "wounding" and "being wounded," perhaps by a particular individual who takes advantage of the absence of light and attacks clandestinely. There is an absence of friends, who may have temporarily deserted because you have not paid them sufficient attention.

The Judgment

Do not simply give up and let yourself be carried away by misfortune. Remain firm and committed – but without being outwardly dogmatic or insisting too strongly on having your own way. Do not allow your inner convictions to become diminished. By all means hide your inner light and vitality under a bushel for now – but remember that the situation is only temporary.

The Image

Be particularly careful of what you say and do. To a certain degree, go with the flow – consider the situation quietly; but neither surrender to plans with which you disagree, nor, for now, reveal them to others. It is judicious to play along, conceal any feelings of opposition, and wait for your moment.

The Lines

1 If you take too strong a line, insisting long and loudly that you are in the right, you will get nowhere. However much other people may put you down, this is not the time to fight them openly.

2 Though these are certainly not comfortable times, you are not seriously injured. Be objective – look at the situation carefully and save what can be saved. Help others in a similar situation if you can.

3 Pure chance will come to the rescue: at the very moment when all your planning seems in vain, a fortunate accident puts you in the position to save the situation.

4 Look for the emergency exit and make use of it. There are some situations too dangerous to face. Get out before the lightning strikes.

5 If you cannot escape from a dangerous position, play dumb and conceal both your own position and any hopes you have of reversing the situation. Be very cautious.

6 It is midnight, and can only get lighter as dawn approaches. At the moment when the darkness is most dense, the sun begins to mount toward the horizon.

37 CHIA JÊN ~ *The Family*

This hexagram is founded on the traditional Chinese family – the father represented by the solid line at the top, and the eldest son by the bottom line. The reference is still often with the family, whether in marriage or in a less formal contract, but it also relates to any group of people in society.

The Judgment

In any social group, strong leadership is required. Hopefully, the sense of authority is founded on affection rather than force. Ideally, the group will mirror the best forms of society, in which those in a position to govern do so in consultation and by persuasion. There should be affection and respect, both from leaders to subordinates and vice versa.

The Image

It is important that you contribute to the running of the group, whether openly or by stealth – perhaps merely by example. Your steadfastness and reliability will be an excellent example, but will also stiffen the backbone of the group as a whole. In a family situation, others will quickly learn to cope with difficult situations by following your behavioral lead.

The Lines

1 The weakest member of the group, the youngest member of the family, must from the beginning be taught to accept authority. Delay this, and there will be difficulties later.

2 The quietest member of the group may be the strongest and most important – in previous generations, the husband was often completely unaware that the wife was ruling the family by stealth.

3 If the leader is too forceful, rebellion is probable. Occasionally a strong hand will be needed, but the best way forward will invariably be by obtaining the consent of all.

4 The control of the purse is always best left to one person – the person who is cleverest at economics (even if he or she is relatively weak within the group).

5 A leader leads best by force of character rather than by force of arms. Respect and affection should not be courted, but won by decent and loving behavior.

6 The well-being of any company depends on its leader; however much he or she consults others, in the end the buck stops at the top, and decisions must be seen to be just.

ABOVE: **Sun**
gentleness, wind/wood, intuition

BELOW: **Li**
fidelity, fire, vision

38 K'UEI ~ *Resistance*

ABOVE: **Li**
fidelity, fire, vision

BELOW: **Tui**
joy, lake, ecstasy

Those who owe allegiance to different people, employers, or ways of life are bound to be more or less antagonistic to each other. Although they may have to find a way of living and working together in moderate harmony, when push comes to shove they will always make decisions on the basis of their fundamental commitment.

The Judgment

Remember that it can be very effective to work with someone whose ideas are opposite to your own. But in order to get the best effect under such circumstances, avoid discussion of big issues and concentrate on small ones. Get those right, and there is always the possibility of reaching a compromise on major issues.

The Image

Fire (the top trigram) and water (the bottom one) do not mix, but one does not necessarily always extinguish or dry up the other – working together in areas that they make their own, they remain individual and retain their specific qualities. Therefore, an emotional, instinctive person can work well with a cold and logical person, provided areas of disagreement are avoided.

The Lines

1 Misunderstandings often resolve themselves if open argument is avoided. Both sides of an argument, well expressed, can be found to be in balance and perfectly compatible.

2 Formal discussion between opposites may result merely in shouting matches. Informal discussions can succeed, provided there is honesty and the intention to make progress.

3 However virulent the opposition or fierce the argument, if a solution must be found it is wise to accept the mud that is thrown at you, ignore it, and press forward.

4 However much you disagree with someone, the conviction that they are honest goes a long way toward building bridges. Examine their motives – but also your own.

5 There is a temptation in certain circumstances to believe that everyone in an opposition group has dishonest motives. This is rarely true. There is usually at least someone you can trust.

6 At any stage of a discussion, the situation can be ruined by misunderstanding. This danger is most acute when you are near to finding a solution.

39 CHIEN ~ *Impediment*

An abyss immediately in front of you and, after you have crossed it, a steep mountain to climb before you reach your goal. But at least these are impediments that can clearly be seen: they are static and will wait while you consider ways of surmounting them. With careful thought, it should be possible to devise ways of overcoming the obstacles in your path.

The Judgment
Do not give up hope. It is important to press ahead, even when the situation seems at its most depressing. Be unswerving in finding and expressing your inner purpose. Consult anyone and everyone who can offer sound advice, and learn from adversity – look upon the trying times ahead as a period during which you can greatly strengthen your mental and physical muscles.

The Image
Standing on the edge of the chasm and looking up at the mountain, it is important to acknowledge that you have made your own way to this point. It is no use blaming other people who may have accompanied you. This is your problem, and yours alone – it is now up to you to solve it.

The Lines
1 It is unwise to take a running jump at the abyss, hoping that you can leap across it. Stop and think: there are easier and safer ways of getting over.

2 Of course you could always give up and turn back. However, there are moral reasons why you should face the danger now – in other words, duty calls.

3 Do not be reckless. Duty may impel you onward, but it could equally call on you, perhaps for the sake of others, to swallow your pride and turn back.

4 You need not stand alone. Others may have crossed the obstacles before you, and be more than willing to offer advice and help.

5 Consider why you feel you must surmount these obstacles. If the reason is truly compelling, muster all your force and don't allow yourself to waver – the goal is worth achieving, and you will succeed.

6 You have seen and evaluated the dangers ahead. It may be that your duty calls you not to conquer them, but to recognize that the peril is too great. Consequently, the only sensible act is to withdraw.

ABOVE: **K'an**
the abyss, water, danger

BELOW: **Kên**
obduracy, mountain, rest

---

40 HSIEH ~ *Release*

ABOVE: **Chên**
exhilaration, thunder, provocation

BELOW: **K'an**
the abyss, water, danger

Although you are not quite out of the woods yet, the situation is at last beginning to move in the right direction. The main obstacle has thankfully been removed – but there are various stages through which you must pass before you are completely free of the difficulties that have dogged you for some time. Consider each of these stages with care, and take a cautious attitude to seemingly obvious solutions.

The Judgment
It is probable that your best course is to return to precisely the position you were in before your present difficulties began. You may be tempted to take advantage of the sudden change and overreach yourself by moving too swiftly ahead. This should certainly be resisted – it would be an error to be premature with the celebrations.

The Image
The mistakes and failures of other people, which have led to difficulties, will now be perfectly clear. Do not harp on about them or insist on pillorying those who made them. Let them go instead – take a relaxed attitude and give everyone the benefit of a clean slate, including yourself.

The Lines
1 When the tension finally subsides, it is important that you too should relax. There is nothing to be said for raking over the ashes. Keep the peace.

2 In the recent past there have been those who have tried to influence you – perhaps by flattery – into taking the wrong course. Now you have found them out, be resolute and firm of purpose.

3 Now that the way ahead seems relatively clear, do not make the mistake of thinking you can close your eyes and take a rest. It is still important to keep your eyes wide open.

4 In order to make progress, you may have found it necessary to become closer than you wanted to some people. You can now distance yourself – but tactfully.

5 If you have decided to break away from colleagues or acquaintances, do so merely by declining their company rather than by insulting or decrying them. Be discreet.

6 There is one more obstacle with which you must deal, possibly a human one. In this case a gentle approach will not work. Be firm, forthright, decisive – and quick.

41 SUN ~ Decline

The Chinese hexagram suggests the weakening of a building by the uncertainty of its foundations, and of wealth reduced by greed. This greed could be other people's or perhaps your own. But money often represents emotion, and the reference can equally be to inner and outer emotion, which may be wasted or overspent.

The Judgment
There are times when an overemotional response is justified and valuable. A speedy and sudden emotional reaction often reveals your innermost heart in an instant. An honest and true response is immediately recognizable, and will invariably turn a situation around.

The Image
It is usually necessary to put a curb on your emotions: they can reveal too much, and frequently show up your weaknesses. Emotion must be consulted to a certain degree, for it is connected with what you feel to be the truth. However, giving your passions full rein can be unwise because they drain your resources. Moderation is the key, and personal restraint prevents other people from taking advantage.

The Lines
1 If someone offers you their unconditional love and help, beware how much use you make of it. You may end up stronger, but at someone else's expense.

2 When your emotions tell you to throw all your resources behind another person, be careful not to overspend – you should not totally exhaust yourself on anyone's behalf.

3 While two is company, three is none. When three people are in a close emotional relationship, jealousy is almost unavoidable. One will simply have to go.

4 Your emotional weakness makes it difficult for others to get close to you. If you are strong and tackle your emotional failings, a richer psychological life will be yours.

5 Do not ignore signs of "good luck." Dismissing them as superstition may be a mistake, for in the past oracles have proved to tell the truth. Without relying on it, accept the promise.

6 Some people seem used by fate to spread their own good fortune among their friends. However chance benefits you, do not forget those around you.

ABOVE: **Kên**
obduracy, mountain, rest

BELOW: **Tui**
joy, lake, ecstasy

42 I ~ Growth

This is one of the seminal hexagrams of the I Ching, expressing the idea that the way to happiness and truth is to be found in the service of others. The emphasis is on spiritual growth, which offers the chief way to developing and fulfilling your own inner being and reaching a balanced and contented relationship with the world. This, in turn, enables you to cope successfully with the problems of life.

The Judgment
Now is a time when you will gain great advantage by making sacrifices for the sake of those who are reliant on you. This opportunity for advancement is only transitory; so grasp it, and make the most of the situation while it lasts. You will find the result rewarding, both in loyalty and in practical service.

The Image
Examine the way those you admire live their lives, and imitate the traits you most esteem. This conscious self-improvement can be compounded by careful consideration of your own personality and actions. Determine to disown and dislodge the characteristics that you realize are damaging your reputation.

The Lines
1 If you suddenly find that someone close to you is in a position to help you take responsibility or grasp an opportunity, accept their help and make full use of it.

2 On the whole, you make your own luck; and at propitious times it seems nothing can injure you. But make no mistakes: a simple slip could undo all your plans.

3 At the moment it seems that even your mistakes turn in your favor. Your authority will be accepted, and you can gain the admiration of those around you.

4 If you are asked for advice, shed all prejudice and regard both friends and foes with a disinterested eye. Ensure that any decision you make is observed by all sides.

5 Be kind and considerate even – or especially – to those you dislike. Act not for the sake of gain, but from an inner conviction that you can see and argue for what is right.

6 It is quite possible that as a result of certain actions – most likely because of selfishness, far too obviously expressed – friends may turn away from you and you will find yourself alone.

ABOVE: **Sun**
gentleness, wood/wind, intuition

BELOW: **Chên**
exhilaration, thunder, provocation

43 KUAI ~ *Progress*

After a long period of tension, suddenly there is a breakthrough and you make progress. After you have steadily stuck to your guns for a long time, opposition suddenly weakens, or even completely disappears. This hexagram is especially strong in springtime, when the frosts die, the air starts to warm, and plants burst into growth.

The Judgment

Make no compromise, but avoid force and depend on persuasion instead. Do not lose yourself in the heat of emotions – be moderate and balanced, and remember that strong passions and cold logic cannot work harmoniously together. Be strong, act with conviction, and acknowledge that you too have failings and weaknesses. It would be an error to disregard your flaws; in theory, they should help you to recognize those of your opponents.

The Image

As the tension rises, recognize that the moment of crisis is approaching. As it gets nearer, be open and relaxed; don't waste energy by resisting the inevitable. Avoid obstinacy, and be prepared to examine and accept the suggestions of others.

The Lines

1 Taking the first step is always difficult. Do so with confidence, but not overconfidence. Avoid thin ice; test the ground before putting your weight on it.

2 The readiness is all. Provided you are vigilant, there is no need for either fear or overconfidence. Coolness and preparation are what is required.

3 You may find yourself on the wrong side of the argument. Do not suddenly withdraw; bide your time, and avoid any situation that will damage you.

4 The disquiet you feel is based on your own inflexibility. Your heart tells you to go one way, but you obstinately stick to the route determined by what seems like "good sense." It may well not be.

5 Once you have followed your heart, and decided on your position, do not withdraw. The Chinese say: once you have decided a weed is a weed, do not hesitate – uproot it.

6 Success at last. But although everything looks perfectly straightforward, there are still lurking nettles. Destroy them before they can cause you any harm.

ABOVE: **Tui**
joy, lake, ecstasy

BELOW: **Ch'ien**
creativity, heaven, strength

44 KOU ~ *Converging*

ABOVE: **Ch'ien**
creativity, heaven, strength

BELOW: **Sun**
gentleness, wood/wind, intuition

The hexagram is associated with the summer solstice. Although it is the height of summer, there is an underlying sense of depression, with the suggestion of approaching autumn and winter. The sunny landscape is shadowed by sudden cloud; possible danger lies ahead, and it is important to recognize it. Think about the consequences, and do your best to avoid them.

The Judgment

Failing to recognize danger, you can sometimes welcome and encourage it. It looks so slight, so insignificant, that it seems silly to fight it. Yet overnight it can grow from a shadow no bigger than one's hand into a thick black cloud darkening the whole landscape. However, if you are certain of someone's good intent, and if you too are free of ulterior motives, meeting each other half-way will have a beneficial result to you both. Anticipation is the key.

The Image

Keep an eye on the general situation. At the moment, you may be so delighted with the progress you have made in one particular area of your life that you miss the signs of impending disaster in another area.

The Lines

1 The Chinese image is of a delightful piglet that grows into a dangerous boar. Notice small things, and anticipate the dangerous course they may take.

2 Nothing in the future seems to offer the kind of hazard that needs to be violently anticipated: given time, a gentle touch is all that will be needed.

3 An easy way presents itself – but has inner dangers. Resist it. Seeing the danger now and taking evasive action will prevent no end of trouble in the near future.

4 You may need the help of someone you would normally regard as useless. At this time you will have to tolerate them and accept their assistance.

5 Let others stride down the road they have chosen, but if you can see that it leads to disaster, warn them gently of the dangers you envisage. Your timely advice should be enough to save them.

6 Who cares what other people say? If you are confident that you are in the right, it may be necessary to accept their scorn. Let it run off your back like rain from a roof.

45 TS'UI ~ *Uniting*

This hexagram is like Pi (*see page 49*), but the sense of vital energy gathering together is even stronger. Ts'ui insists that it is absolutely necessary for you not to work alone. It implores you to seek out people who might be of help, and to cooperate with them in every conceivable way in order to resolve the situation in which you find yourself – whether this problem is of a personal or a professional nature.

The Judgment
You can look for help either from your family, friends, or colleagues; you can lead in discussion or action, or rely on the intelligence and wisdom of someone in whom you trust. But first, you must be collected and at peace within yourself. If you are trustful, the result will be positive.

The Image
Gathering together in a group is an act of unity, but with many personalities confined to one place, conflicts are likely to occur. Unvoiced differences and fractious exchanges weaken any group, making it difficult to deal with sudden emergencies or events. Try to foresee areas of difficulty, and prepare to deal with them the moment they occur.

The Lines
1 Group discussion is important, but in the end one person is the leader, and it is up to him or her to make the final decision. The other group members must simply accept it.

2 After separate opinions have been given, a general consensus will emerge; and it is important for the group leader to accept this rather than trying to influence it.

3 Occasionally circumstances or personalities will exclude you from a group. The solution is often to befriend a particular member, preferably an important one, and work through him or her.

4 Take particular notice of one person who stands at the center of the problem you are facing: he or she may be friend or foe, but nevertheless holds the key to the future.

5 A group sometimes centers on one particular person because of his or her influential position, rather than a more solid reason. It may be necessary to criticize.

6 If you are misunderstood by an important colleague, show how much you regret the misunderstanding; this will convince much more strongly than any argument.

ABOVE: **Tui**
joy, lake, ecstasy

BELOW: **K'un**
flexibility, earth, adaptability

46 SHÊNG ~ *Aspiration*

ABOVE: **K'un**
flexibility, earth, adaptability

BELOW: **Sun**
gentleness, wind/wood, intuition

The hexagram Shêng concentrates on sheer natural willpower. This power is not consciously exerted – instead it is inherent in a person so that he or she is apparently forced to succeed by some inward force almost beyond his or her control. It is the type of willpower that provides some people with the energy and drive necessary to run worldwide conglomerates, lead nations, and make great conquests.

The Judgment
Success is the result of talent, expressed without self-consciousness, with simplicity and often great charm. Energy also has a significant role to play – you may be lucky, but the harder you work, the luckier you are likely to become. Seeking the support of influential people is encouraged – there is no need to be wary of them, because mutual success is assured.

The Image
Success comes as naturally as the leaf to the tree, and grows steadily and ceaselessly. Everything is as it should be. If you are adaptable and flexible in outlook, and inexhaustible in energy, you will press constantly onward.

The Lines
1 This is the beginning. Your absolute conviction that you are on the right path will result in progress; but look to other people, including your colleagues, for their support and approval.

2 You are not in an ideal situation. If you are strong but not too blunt, your lack of sympathy with others should do you no lasting harm.

3 This is a time of considerable success, when obstacles suddenly fall away. This happy state of affairs will not last forever – ensure that you use this time wisely.

4 At last your efforts have been successful, and you are accepted by your peers. Enjoy this moment while it lasts – it is possible that your status may be at an all-time high.

5 Do not lose your head over your present success, and do not be tempted to overreach yourself. Although you may feel indomitable, a leap in the dark could land you in trouble.

6 Be careful: however strong, confident, and powerful you feel, striding forward incautiously in pitch darkness can only have one result – disaster.

47 K'UN ~ *Persecution*

This is a time of exhaustion, oppression, and restraint, which can make you subject to feelings of persecution or repression. Someone you consider repugnant will get in your way, and may even restrict your progress for some little time. The situation will not be permanent, but it may be some time before you can free yourself from the person who is holding you back.

The Judgment
Good humor in the face of adversity is the key to success. Remember that even repression can lead to advantage, for the energy you must muster to overcome it may kick-start you into action for which you have not had the stomach until now. Plan carefully and remain optimistic. Don't waste time trying to explain yourself – you will need to retain as much of your inner strength as possible. Keep your eye on the goal.

The Image
The Chinese image is of a dried-up and exhausted lake. This may be similar to how you feel, and indeed the future may look arid. Accept the position, but retain your natural optimism and strength of purpose. The rains will eventually come.

The Lines
1 Meet trouble head-on, recognize it, and resolve to use all your strength to overcome it. Any tendency to feel that you are beaten only saps the strength you will need to climb out of the pit.

2 Even though you have enough to eat and drink, and have somewhere to live, you may feel deeply depressed at the moment. Think positively and be patient.

3 Some people like banging their heads against a wall because it's so nice when they stop. This is pointless – don't allow yourself to be oppressed by minor issues.

4 You may realize that you have made a mistake. Happily, the result will not be calamitous – you have the strength to correct the error and reverse any disadvantage.

5 You may be discouraged because the very people you had counted on to help you have proved disinclined or useless. Little by little things will right themselves.

6 Difficulties begin to resolve themselves. You may be uncertain how to proceed. Seize the opportunity to disentangle yourself from the situation, and be firm of purpose.

ABOVE: **Tui**
joy, lake, ecstasy

BELOW: **K'an**
the abyss, water, danger

48 CHING ~ *The Well*

This hexagram is one of only two in the I Ching that represents a material object – here, the Well. (The other is No. 50, Ting, the Cooking Pot.) Ching is associated with well water, which is drawn up by wooden poles – that is, the means by which humankind draws the means of survival from the earth. The hexagram also refers to the natural world – plants extend their roots into the ground to draw up water for growth. We associate water with our deepest emotions, and Ching can be seen as representing our search for emotional nourishment.

The Judgment
However sophisticated our life and surroundings, we all have the same need to express and satisfy our emotions, and fulfill ourselves as human beings. Economic and worldly success can sometimes make us smug and lazy; such neglect is damaging and prevents our self-development.

The Image
Just as a bucket draws water from a well, so men and women draw on personal emotional resources not only to nurture themselves but also to enrich the lives of others, and to draw society together in mutual fellowship.

The Lines
1 If you neglect yourself you cannot expect to be respected or admired by others. If you lose respect, you also lose influence and become insignificant.

2 People who fail to use their talents are in the end ignored by their peers, and have to turn for fellowship to their intellectual inferiors. This results in their minds being dulled even further.

3 You have intelligence, knowledge, and wit, and yet are ignored by those with whom you wish to associate. At present, there is nothing to be done about this.

4 You seem to be facing a blank wall, unable to make progress. Use the time to put your own affairs in order, and prepare for the time when you can again move forward.

5 Do not ignore the words and actions of the excellent men and women around you. Be prepared to learn from them, and spread their good example to others.

6 The more open you are, and the more you give emotionally to those around you, the more highly you will be regarded. Remember that the well of emotion never runs dry.

ABOVE: **K'an**
the abyss, water, danger

BELOW: **Sun**
gentleness, wind/wood, intuition

49 KO ~ *Upheaval*

The Chinese hexagram refers to an animal that is molting – losing its pelt and changing its appearance in the process. Similarly, human institutions frequently lose their accustomed image and are subject to change. This can happen to individuals, too; but their unfamiliarity in their new guise can give rise to antagonism, and like the fire and water of the hexagram, to mutual opposition.

The Judgment
Avoid serious upheavals unless the situation is so grave that nothing else will do. The time must be right, and any drastic changes need to be truly for the general good. Think of others as well as yourself, because selfishness is likely to lead to regretting the action later. Change is natural – there are different seasons in your life, as well as in nature.

The Image
Light and dark battle throughout the year as a matter of course – the four seasons, which mark the passage of time, are the result. Fire and water destroy each other. Try to see change as inevitable, and some destruction as unavoidable. Look ahead, see the changes coming, and adjust to them through anticipation and planning.

The Lines
1 Be patient and restrain yourself. Only insist upon drastic change and upheaval when there is nothing else to be done. Premature action will result in disaster.

2 If change is unavoidable, plan carefully for it. Think about the result of the change you are considering, and prepare yourself for the new circumstances.

3 Avoid haste and ruthlessness, but also procrastination and doubt. Some changes are best avoided, others are inevitable. It is important to distinguish between them.

4 Do you have the strength of purpose to carry out radical change? Do you possess inner conviction and determination, too? Be truthful – do not merely give the answer that you want to hear.

5 Make your intentions perfectly clear. There should be no doubt about the way you are going, and any possible detours or bypasses should be blocked from the start.

6 One change, no matter how major, may not solve the whole situation. Some fine-tuning usually becomes necessary, which may involve an element of backtracking.

ABOVE: **Tui**
joy, lake, ecstasy

BELOW: **Li**
fidelity, fire, vision

50 TING ~ *The Cooking Pot*

This hexagram is one of only two in the I Ching that represents a material object, here the Cooking Pot, rather than an abstract image. (The other is No. 48, Ching, the Well.) In China, the ritual vessel known as the *ting* held the cooked meats in the ancestors' temple. Consequently, the hexagram is associated with emotional nourishment. A cooking pot is used to prepare food, so here the reference is also to strengthening your emotional resources to nourish not only yourself but others.

The Judgment
The wood at the bottom of the hexagram fuels the fire at the top. This is a reference to the inner resources that nurture your outward dealings with the world, and to the many spiritual assets upon which you can draw when feeling under pressure.

The Image
The idea of fate is not one that should depress you. If you believe that your life is "fated," you should strive to balance the inevitable with your sense of the purpose of your life. The challenge here is not simply to resign yourself to your fate but to work diligently to enhance it.

The Lines
1 Everyone can be "a success" in one sense or another. It is important to "know our place" – not so that we can resign ourselves to it, but so that we can climb as high as possible from it.

2 Do not overreach yourself. Although it is always important to strive, it should not be beyond what good sense tells you, because that would be a waste of effort.

3 Inner conviction will eventually become outward success. If you are unrecognized at present, bide your time – real quality is always eventually acknowledged.

4 If you are faced with a task beyond your strength, you may be tempted to take half-hearted measures just to keep yourself afloat without striving to reach the shore.

5 If you are modest and strong, you will attract many admirers, all eager to offer their support. When that happens, modesty should not prevent you from remaining the leader.

6 A great leader is likened to jade, combining purity with strength. Mildness of manner and strength of purpose is a potent combination that is impossible to resist.

ABOVE: **Li**
fidelity, fire, vision

BELOW: **Sun**
gentleness, wind/wood, intuition

51 CHÊN ~ *Stimulation*

The exhilaration of a thunderstorm is both shocking and exciting – it can be literally earth-shattering and cause great fear, leaving you shaken and distressed. But it also lifts thick and depressing atmospheres, and leaves clarity, lightness, and purity behind it. This hexagram indicates something so terrifying and violent as to be almost uncontrollable.

The Judgment
Your innermost thoughts, instincts, and emotions can be frightening in their intensity when their force is fully released. But once they have been acknowledged and expressed, they lose their cumulative power. Repressing them makes them all the stronger, and you will suffer from the strain. If you retain your composure, do not allow yourself to be distracted, and try to come to terms with your emotions, you will eventually be able to control and direct them to your advantage.

The Image
Even if you are appalled by what you discover when you look honestly into your own motives, you must learn to respect them, to control them when they can do you harm, and to encourage them when they elevate and expand your mind.

The Lines
1 You may be so shaken by the emotional storm that you feel unequal to dealing with others, and are thus at a disadvantage. But self-knowledge is always an invaluable tool, to be used in the present or the future.

2 Accept loss philosophically and without worrying too much about it. Things are only things; money is only money. What is important remains.

3 The shock you suffer at present is external, so ultimately unimportant; no real damage has been done. Maintain your balance – you still have all your faculties.

4 Stand still. You cannot fight, for there is nothing to fight; yet there seems no path you can follow. Accept the position and wait patiently for change.

5 Not one shock, but several. Sway with the movement, absorb the jolts, and retain your self-possession until the storms have passed.

6 You are probably still in a state of shock. Make no decision until you have recovered your self-confidence – and take care that others around you do not infect you with their fear or nervousness.

ABOVE: **Chên**
exhilaration, thunder, provocation

BELOW: **Chên**
exhilaration, thunder, provocation

52 KÊN ~ *Self-possession*

ABOVE: **Kên**
obduracy, mountain, rest

BELOW: **Kên**
obduracy, mountain, rest

This is a hexagram of tremendous firmness and self-possession. It represents not only the person who possesses these qualities, but also those who strive to attain them. It speaks of calmness – of those whose firmness is expressed without a loud voice or an ostentatious manner, are well-balanced in themselves, and seek to promote balance in every situation.

The Judgment
Rest is the complementary opposite of movement. Both are necessary for inner balance and harmony. Act from a position of true peace of mind – move when the moment is opportune, and remain still and quiet when it is not. A quiet, measured look at the most difficult situation can reveal the still center from which it can be controlled. Having achieved that calmness, it is impossible to make mistakes.

The Image
Discipline your mind so that it does not wander: it is important to concentrate on a problem without allowing yourself to be distracted by irrelevant thoughts. The kind of mind that wanders aimlessly only makes confusion more confused.

The Lines
1 Stop, look, and listen before you make a move! Once involved in a problem, it is difficult to see it clearly and to stop your mind from aimless deviation.

2 If the person in control has already made the wrong decision and is sweeping down the wrong road, there may be nothing you can do except try to avoid personal calamity.

3 At the moment, you should perhaps allow yourself to float with the current. But remain in control – wear a lifejacket if necessary, but do not swim in any particular direction.

4 Try to distance yourself completely from any difficulty with which you are surrounded. This may not be entirely possible, but at least avoid getting personally involved.

5 Now is not a time for free speech: an indiscreet word could land you in real difficulty. Remember that discretion can easily be mistaken for wisdom, and will not get you into trouble.

6 Strive for complete inactivity – make no rash movement – indeed make no movement at all. Even thinking too much about the situation may be worrying, so be tranquil.

53 CHIEN ~ *Evolution*

Slow, careful, well-prepared, and deliberate progress is indicated here. Proceed gradually, step by step, and test the tightrope before you put all your weight on it. Depend upon the sense of balance that you have cultivated, and do not make any rash movement that could endanger either you or the plans that you have made.

The Judgment

If you act in haste, you will repent at leisure. Cultivate calmness and tranquillity instead, which will enable you to look at your circumstances without agitation or hysteria and see them clearly. Do not try to solve any major problem in the blink of an eye – take your time. It would be a waste of effort to spend your energy in self-promotion – the best influence on other people will be your good example. Gradual progress will be yours, but only if you persevere.

The Image

If you are to be taken seriously, you need a certain weight and gravitas. No one is eager to follow a fool, or even someone who does not seem to be fully in command of the situation. Personal development is the key to influencing others.

The Lines

1 You may find yourself isolated and alone, under the impression that everyone around is watching you carefully and waiting for your first move. That move should be very cautious indeed.

2 If you are the fortunate one, share your good fortune with others. Circumstances have arisen, and will arise again, when you will be grateful for others' generosity.

3 Jumping in at the deep end is unwise, especially if you are not a strong swimmer. Take your time, and wait calmly until you can see a realistic way forward.

4 If you are in a dangerous situation, withdrawal may be the only way toward eventual progress. Bend with the wind, yield, and rest in safety until the danger passes.

5 Those closest to you may unjustly suspect you – perhaps because someone has been spreading lies. Such misjudgments will be corrected in time.

6 The task is nearing completion. One more step – and you may take that step with confidence. Others will admire the example of your success.

ABOVE: **Sun**
gentleness, wind/wood, intuition

BELOW: **Kên**
obduracy, mountain, rest

54 KUEI MEI ~ *Guidance*

The hexagram tells of a young girl married to an older man who devotes himself to her education. It underlines the principle of people leading each other by example and teaching, mutual assistance, and working together for the advancement of society and the good of every member of it.

The Judgment

Overreaching yourself will lead to strife and discord with others. Work for the common good rather than for personal benefit, and take your place in the scheme of things. Accept the limitations of your position – there are benefits, but it is up to you to discover them. Formal contracts may be necessary between people for legal reasons, but the best form of contract is voluntary: "duty" and "rights" then fail to exist, for the mutual respect of one for the other results in total trust and affection.

The Image

Misunderstanding and disagreement can affect any relationship. Allowing the relationship to drift can encourage this; a strong mutual sense of purpose, knowing just where you want to go, will avoid it. Keep the end firmly in sight and work toward it.

The Lines

1 It is the time to be the power behind the throne. If someone has asked for your help, give it freely, accept the confidence, but be tactful in the assistance you give.

2 Although your loss can never be entirely healed, if you retain loyalty and your sense of good faith, it should be possible to continue regardless of misfortune.

3 It is a mistake to live entirely on hope: pie in the sky does not fill the stomach. There is little to be done at the moment – so do not make promises that cannot be fulfilled.

4 Your sense of honor or of right and wrong prevents you from joining in a particular action. Do what you think is proper; your reward will come.

5 It is important to recognize that sometimes you must accept a subordinate position. It is usually possible to have considerable influence from a seemingly lowly position.

6 Do not take some action because it is popular, or just because it is "the right thing to do." If you are convinced that the action is worthless or even improper, it is not only futile but dangerous.

ABOVE: **Chên**
exhilaration, thunder, provocation

BELOW: **Tui**
joy, lake, ecstasy

55 FÊNG ~ *Plenty*

Here is the suggestion of a very civilized life, free of both passion and undue difficulty, supported by adequate means, and tending toward luxury and comfort. But, as with all situations, it cannot remain static – it must, according to the laws of nature, change. Acknowledge that this is the apogee, and that the only way to go from here is down. How long you manage to sustain your position or delay your descent from it depends largely upon your probity and faithfulness.

The Judgment

The person who has everything is in a dangerous position, for there is ample opportunity to spoil things – by mean actions, bad motives, idleness, and lack of care. Therefore it is important to live fully for the moment, and free yourself from the tensions and anxieties that hold you back from fulfilment. The knowledge that this golden time cannot continue forever should not spoil your enjoyment of it.

The Image

Thunder above, lightning (fire) below. Thorough investigation and punishment of some kind is in the air. If you must inflict the punishment, do not be too forceful.

The Lines

1 Two people brought together by the same ambition and sharing the same objectives can scarcely fail to work well. Make the most of the opportunity.

2 Like-minded people can be driven apart by intrigues: make sure your motives are clear and your mind is open. Beware of any feelings of mistrust and envy.

3 If you have broken a limb, it must be rested. This is not the time for vigorous action. Wait until the bone heals and the muscle has been restrengthened.

4 The light in the east is indeed the dawn; but have the patience to wait until you can see clearly before making a move, then everything will go well.

5 If you have been modest and just in your dealings, those who know you will be honest in giving their opinions and offering their help, and you can only profit from it.

6 Arrogantly seeking out position and profit invariably results in the exact opposite of what is most desired – the alienation of not only strangers but also respected colleagues, and well-loved family and friends.

ABOVE: **Chên**
exhilaration, thunder, provocation

BELOW: **Li**
fidelity, fire, vision

---

56 LÜ ~ *Traveler*

ABOVE: **Li**
fidelity, fire, vision

BELOW: **Kên**
obduracy, mountain, rest

Some people are perpetual travelers. They have decided for one reason or another that wandering around from town to town, even country to country, is the best way of satisfying their inner selves, and of living their life. Travelers need to have a strong character – as well as avoiding the constraints of society, they manage to live without society's support.

The Judgment

Broadening your horizons is an invaluable experience, but try not to allow your love of independence to alienate you from society or from those who do not share your tastes. Live your own inner life by all means; but be aware of life going on outside your experience, too. Carefully examine the motives of those you meet on the road – the most stable, secure part of your life is your sense of yourself, and it is up to you to have the strength of character not to be led astray.

The Image

The Chinese image is of a prison, but one that is only temporary. Detachment from the world around you should be merely a transitory state – if it becomes permanent, isolation will result in complete detachment from human emotion.

The Lines

1 The more that others sneer or patronize you, the more important it is to maintain a sense of dignity and self-possession. Do not attempt to obtain respect by retreating from your position.

2 If you show other people that you trust them, they, in turn, will trust you. If you are the one in search of favor, do so by showing modesty and dignity.

3 If you allow yourself to be irritated by others to the point of anger, or to be driven to arrogance and trespassing, your situation will become dangerous.

4 A wanderer in a foreign land will never feel completely at ease – he or she must always be on guard, and be prepared to respect the customs of the host.

5 There are ways to penetrate even the most alien situation. There are no people in the world so hostile that they cannot be coaxed into friendship by the correct means.

6 Speech is not something to be used carelessly. In a difficult and alien situation, language is at once a gift and a danger: it must always be used prudently.

57 SUN ~ *Shrewdness*

Shrewdness is a quality that prevents us from falling into traps or becoming entangled in problems through failing to appreciate the inherent difficulties of a situation. Cultivating clear, penetrating insight not only enables us to stay out of trouble, but also equips us to advise other people who find themselves in similar predicaments.

The Judgment

Shrewdness does not show itself in sudden thoughts or actions. It is a calm, acute state of mind that must be gradually acquired and evenly expressed. This ability is at its most effective when it is used to approach and reach a particular goal.

The Image

Be clear and resolute in your own mind. Only when you know what is to be done should it be put into place – action should always follow the shrewd assessment of a situation. Acting without foresight is foolhardy, and will end in disaster. "Playing it by ear" is something that may be all very well where music is concerned, but which is all too often a mistake when coping with difficult situations. Shrewd judgment is the much better course.

The Lines

1 Although gentleness is undoubtedly a fine quality, events too often fail to respond to a gentle approach. Now is the time for decisiveness and resolution.

2 Opposition should be traced back to its base. Shrewd observation of the people concerned, and the circumstances in which they are acting, is the only way of doing this.

3 It is a mistake to think about a situation to the point of exhaustion. There comes a moment when you know as much as you need to know before you act.

4 Examine your position carefully. If you feel secure, and are sure that the information you have enables you to make a shrewd assessment of the action you need to take, the time is right.

5 Things may not have gone well, and this may be the time to change your approach. Think carefully, and when you have acted, watch the results and fine-tune if necessary.

6 Having examined a situation with the utmost care, it is sometimes the case that for now you have to leave well enough alone. Delay is the best course.

ABOVE: **Sun**
gentleness, wind/wood, intuition

BELOW: **Sun**
gentleness, wind/wood, intuition

58 TUI ~ *Happiness*

ABOVE: **Tui**
joy, lake, ecstasy

BELOW: **Tui**
joy, lake, ecstasy

Although the quality of the trigram Tui is "ecstasy," the hexagram is associated with a quieter emotion founded on inner strength, steadfastness, and tenderness. True and lasting happiness is founded on deeper qualities than abandon and exhilaration; love may be a passion, but passion need not necessarily be part of love.

The Judgment

Sheer strength of will, perhaps to the extent of intimidation, will certainly have an effect; but it will not last for long. Kindness, gentleness, and friendliness are the keys to lasting influence and support. In the same way, love without affection can have moments of great enjoyment; but it is invariably transitory. When gentleness plays its part, it lays the foundation for lasting partnership – just as friendship is the best basis for social success.

The Image

Knowledge and experience should be shared for the common good – open your heart to those from whom you can learn. The company of friends is most valuable when you can discuss anything with them, without reticence or fear.

The Lines

1 The man or woman who is truly happy has a quiet security that nothing can shake: to desire nothing is to be content.

2 Yielding to the temptation to enjoy pleasures that the heart tells you are unworthy leads to remorse and unhappiness. Do not succumb.

3 Self-indulgence is easy – there are so many idle delights with which to pass the time. But time passes very quickly: do you want to race toward its end?

4 Consider what gives you innermost pleasure. Torn between real happiness and what brings temporary gratification, is there really any choice?

5 Yielding to temptation just once surely cannot be so bad? But once in a lifetime? Once a month? Soon, once a week. There is only one place that this can end – it is a dangerous and downward path.

6 Chasing after pleasure is an enjoyable way of forgetting your troubles, but not of dealing with them. Allowing weakness and vanity to rule, and refusing to take control of your life, will invariably end in disaster.

59 HUAN ~ *Dispersion*

Inner tension often results in the inability to show emotion, to express yourself freely, and to communicate readily not only with partners, but also with society at large. Calmness and gentleness will disperse the blockage, not force of will. It is important to learn to release tension (by meditation, exercise, or whatever means is most suitable to you) and thus allow your intimate self room to breathe and expand.

The Judgment
Being a member of a group – part of something larger than yourself – can be very powerful and rewarding. The inability to be part of something, show love, or even care for others, is often founded on egotism. It is important to dissolve this: when you are free of self you are able to be part of society rather than living within a selfish cocoon.

The Image
A sense of fellowship is immensely important for development. Religion and art are two of the most effective means of getting in touch with the highest ideals of humankind, losing the sense of yourself as all-important, and learning to cope with the difficult ideas of eternity and a limitless universe.

The Lines
1 Be open and relaxed – confront any disagreement and discord the moment it begins, and disperse any anger or irritation calmly and with gentle but firm action.

2 When feelings of injustice, cynicism, or bad temper begin to set you apart from others, they should be speedily dispersed. If these feelings are allowed to fester, they will destroy.

3 Problems can sometimes be too great to solve by private action; close friends and colleagues must be trusted to offer advice and practical help.

4 Private opinion must be set aside when circumstances demand an objective, wider view of any problem. Remember that there are circumstances when loyalty to colleagues and even partners is misplaced.

5 Just a single idea, quickly put into action, can save the most complex of situations. Hesitation and procrastination disperses the energy necessary for success.

6 Do the right thing, for others as well as yourself – do not leap into the lifeboat alone. Help others to escape danger before you think of saving yourself.

ABOVE: **Sun**
gentleness, wind/wood, intuition

BELOW: **K'an**
the abyss, water, danger

60 CHIEH ~ *Constraint*

ABOVE: **K'an**
the abyss, water, danger

BELOW: **Tui**
joy, lake, ecstasy

Limits and boundaries are not purely restrictive – they also give shape and substance. In every area of life, whether in finance, love, business, or exercise, there is a limit beyond which it is unwise to go. The setting of that limit should not be entrusted to others: only you know the point beyond which your muscles will tear, your bank balance go into the red, or your beloved be unable to bear the weight of dependence.

The Judgment
Although limits even exist in nature – the seasons change from one to another at a relatively fixed time – moderation is the key, even to constraint. Allowing the full expression of self is necessary, but knowing just the point at which to stop is equally important. Restraint when times are good means that it is easier to live when times are difficult – and this applies in any area of life.

The Image
Disaster awaits the rich, able to indulge themselves limitlessly: this leads to disenchantment and finally to boredom. Good judgment tells you when to stop, and learning discrimination and when to obey it leads to a well-balanced and happy life.

The Lines
1 Knowing your limits – and abiding by them – leads to eventual success. There is a time to speak and a time to be silent. Discretion is the key.

2 Until the moment has come to speak out, be silent. Until the moment has come for action, be still. Hesitation is an art. But when the time is right, make your move. Do not miss your opportunity.

3 "Have your fun – and pay for it." The fee can be so high that it is crippling. Constraint results in always being able to pay your bills.

4 The inner battle to restrain yourself is sometimes so bitter that it saps your energy. It is therefore all the more important to learn the art of restraint as early as possible, so that energy can then be more efficiently used.

5 Do not urge restraint on others before you have learned it yourself. Your own modesty should be the example that enables you to urge others in the same direction.

6 If you are too severe, your restrictions are likely to end in rebellion. A ruthless approach is sometimes the only recourse. But this situation should not last for long.

61 CHUNG FU ~ *Confidence*

This hexagram concentrates on social position. In some ways it is now outmoded; but even in the most egalitarian society, we are "above" some people and "below" others, at least in financial terms. Everyone has a position in society that is different from other people's in terms of preferences, inclinations, tastes, and behavior. We must all be at ease in this area of our lives.

The Judgment
The Judgment compares pigs and fish – both part of nature but essentially very different creatures. When we are dealing with people who are different from us, we need to disregard our prejudices and rely on common humanity to establish a mutual bond between us. If human contact is based on inner truth and what is right and pure, good fortune is ensured for all concerned.

The Image
Puzzled disapproval achieves nothing. If it is difficult to understand someone or their actions, respond humanely; and try to put yourself in their place without consciously attempting to analyze them or their motives. The results are likely to be understanding, sympathy, and empathy.

The Lines
1 Secret alliances with others never help to solve a situation, but lead to complications and betrayals. Rely on your own powers of analysis instead.

2 Some people influence others by the sheer power of their personality and the simple expression of their goodness and openness. This gradually wears away opposition as water wears away stone.

3 Those we love have the most influence upon us. Whether we allow this to sway our lives or not depends on the relationship – but it is important to recognize the fact.

4 We can learn much from our "superiors" – those who know more and are more successful than us. The lessons can only be learned, however, if we are modest.

5 The power of personality cannot be over-valued. Someone who has to "rule" other people will find strength of character their best instrument.

6 Words are important, but in the end they are only words. Only if they are backed by rigorous thought and faith in their truth will they have any lasting effect.

ABOVE: **Sun**
gentleness, wind/wood, intuition

BELOW: **Tui**
joy, lake, ecstasy

62 HSIAO KUO ~ *Small is Beautiful*

ABOVE: **Chên**
exhilaration, thunder, provocation

BELOW: **Kên**
the abyss, water, danger

It is important to acknowledge the areas of life with which you are least able to deal successfully. Even the most eminent people have their weaknesses, and by understanding them they can deal with them. If you are in a position of power and influence, but do not realize the aspects of that position where difficulty is likely to arise, there is always likely to be trouble.

The Judgment
Modesty is an excellent quality, but only when it is real. False modesty, assumed to impress other people, is a weakness, and sometimes leads you into a position where it is suddenly impossible to exert the influence and use the power that is necessary. Do not become overimpressed by the power of your position. Stick with what you know, and do your best with it – now is not the time to be furthering your aspirations.

The Image
The more powerful a person is, the more important it is to fix the mind conscientiously on correct behavior and duty. Openness and lack of pretense strengthen your position; it is important to be humble and on the side of the underdog.

The Lines
1 Do not take exceptional measures until they are absolutely necessary. Even when they are necessary, make sure that you have the power to act before making a move.

2 Even when you know that you are in the right, it is sometimes politic to swallow pride and continue to work as instructed. The fault is then not yours.

3 When discretion is necessary, it can be dangerous to ignore the dangers and carry on as if there is no problem. Paying attention to small details can help.

4 Take great care. Perseverance is the right road to take, but with caution and without undue pressure on those who take a different view than you.

5 Never hesitate to seek advice from the wise, even if they are outside your own sphere. Look for people who possess real knowledge, and whose experience qualifies them to enlighten you.

6 Do not press on regardless. Take particular notice of important small details which, though they appear insignificant, may hold the key to the situation.

63 CHI CHI ~ *Tough at the Top*

Everything is in a state of perfect balance – but the slightest movement can cause imminent collapse. It is just when you seem to have solved the problem, when the danger seems past, when you seem secure, that you can lose everything by making a false move. Any rash decision can prove disastrous, and the elation of victory can deprive you of the cool judgment that is necessary to consolidate your triumph and ensure future good fortune. Only proceed with extreme caution.

The Judgment

It may seem to be a time when you can freewheel, relax, and ignore small details in the overall good fortune. It is unrealistic to expect everything simply to turn out for the best. Detachment is as ill-advised now as at the most difficult moments; continue to be cautious and watchful.

The Image

In the midst of success and comfort, do not relax unduly because at last you have got what you want. Recognize the moments when failing to pay attention to detail may start a small fire that can consume everything for which you have worked. Be vigilant and watchful in your actions.

The Lines

1 Have a drink with friends, certainly, but do not take one too many, and do not lower your guard. Do not allow celebrations to distract you from business.

2 Having reached a safe plateau, do not cause trouble by embarking immediately upon another perhaps perilous climb to new heights. Take your time; survey the ground.

3 The urge to go further, to climb higher, is understandable, but recognize that you may be embarking on a much longer, harder journey than you have prepared for.

4 A small mistake may seem large enough to spoil a victory. Do not allow it to distract you. Take it as a warning, be more careful, but do not anticipate disgrace or failure.

5 Outward displays of success may mislead some people, and temporarily succeed in giving you a position you do not merit. In the end, however, you will be tested.

6 It is always pleasant to celebrate success by looking back at those you have passed in the race. While you are standing still, admiring your victory, beware of someone catching you up on your blind side.

ABOVE: **K'an**
the abyss, water, danger

BELOW: **Li**
fidelity, fire, vision

64 WEI CHI ~ *The Final Step*

The final hexagram of the I Ching has an optimistic outlook – spring has arrived, the ice has melted, the ground is beginning to warm, and the first indications of life are returning. The situation seems at last to be under control. However, there are still one or two steps to be taken to ensure success; make sure that all loose ends have been addressed, and that there is no way in which former problems can recur.

The Judgment

Difficulties may still lie ahead, but with decisions made and a definite and distinctive goal in prospect, it is now possible to make real progress, moving purposefully and with caution, making no last-minute error. When the prospects of success are so likely, it would be a shame to allow your lack of experience to lead you into trouble – seek guidance from those who can help you.

The Image

Make sure you know precisely what you want and precisely what you are doing. It is only when you are centered and calm in your mind, and quite sure of your situation, that you can embark on the action which will lead to lasting success and tranquillity.

ABOVE: **Li**
fidelity, fire, vision

BELOW: **K'an**
the abyss, water, danger

The Lines

1 Once you see the goal within reach, it is tempting to race for it at full speed. However, tripping up when moving too quickly can result in permanent damage.

2 Patience does not mean standing still and doing nothing. In this instance, patience refers to moving carefully, making slow, steady progress, and keeping a firm hand on the handbrake.

3 If the final, conclusive effort seems beyond your strength, now is the time to look around for outside help from trusted friends rather than completely exhausting yourself.

4 It is now or never. Forget any qualms, forge ahead, and lay firm foundations for future security, whether in your personal or professional life.

5 Complete and unqualified success after a tough struggle offers you all the good fortune that you could wish for, enjoyed all the more for its contrast with the past.

6 Celebration is certainly in order, but at the same time should be kept within bounds. Triumphalism should be avoided: only the fool will shout "Rejoice! Rejoice!"

I CHING – TWO CASE HISTORIES

When you consult the *I Ching*, some statements, whether in the Judgment, the Image, or the Lines, will seem to have an obvious bearing on the question, while others may seem to be irrelevant. Do not ignore the so-called "irrelevant" statements – they often throw an illuminating sideways glance on the situation, and are invariably more revealing than they at first appear.

A QUESTION OF PROMOTION

THE BACKGROUND

Ed has applied for promotion at work and is in competition with Josh, his colleague. When comparing himself to Josh, Ed considers himself to be more highly skilled, better educated, and more thorough, but does admit that Josh's approach appears to be more slick. Josh has had several successes lately, which have undermined Ed's self-confidence. But Ed consoles himself with the belief that Josh's successes are based on ideas that are flashy, but in the end unsound. Ed's question for the *I Ching* is, "What attitude should I take at my interview for promotion?"

THE COINS	THE SCORES	THE LINES
	$2 + 2 + 2 = 6$	──x── *(line 1)*
	$2 + 3 + 2 = 7$	────── *(line 2)*
	$3 + 3 + 2 = 8$	── ── *(line 3)*
	$3 + 2 + 2 = 7$	────── *(line 4)*
	$2 + 2 + 3 = 7$	────── *(line 5)*
	$2 + 3 + 2 = 7$	────── *(line 6)*

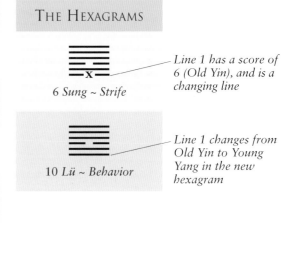

THE HEXAGRAMS

6 Sung ~ Strife — Line 1 has a score of 6 (Old Yin), and is a changing line

10 Lü ~ Behavior — Line 1 changes from Old Yin to Young Yang in the new hexagram

THE ANSWER

The throws of the Chinese coins resulted in hexagram No. 6, Sung, Strife (*see page 48*). This hexagram underlines the unspoken antagonism and sense of separation between the two men, and recognizes that there might be trouble ahead. At the interview, Ed should certainly resist the temptation to denigrate Josh's concepts. Instead, he should be confident in his own experience and achievement, and make sure that his worth is realized by other people ("If you are in the right, then all is well and you can relax"). He should be moderate and balanced, and not allow his desire for promotion to become the be-all and end-all of his life ("Keep a clear, honest head at all times" and "Think through the situation slowly and carefully").

Line one of Sung is a changing line (Old Yin), indicating that Ed should pay particular attention to this line. It underlines the fact that while Ed might have to accept a temporary setback, all will eventually be well ("There may be trouble, but things will finally turn out to your advantage").

In the new hexagram, line one (Old Yin) changes to Young Yang. The resulting hexagram is No. 10, Lü, Behavior (*see page 50*). Line one of the new hexagram refers to Josh and warns Ed against automatically assuming that Josh is inferior to him ("Class, in the old sense of the word, is dead"). Nevertheless, the last line still promises ultimate success for Ed ("If it has ended well, the result will be positive – but no one will know but yourself").

A MATTER OF THE HEART

THE BACKGROUND

Anne has been married to her husband, Terry, for twelve years. Their marriage has been happy, and Anne still loves Terry; but his libido has faltered recently, and their sex life has become unfulfilling and dull as a result. Bruce, the brother of one of Anne's best friends, has made a determined pass at her, and has suggested that they should enjoy an uncomplicated, "no strings" sexual relationship. Bruce is considerably younger than Anne, and

handsome and in good shape. Anne finds Bruce sexually exciting, and is flattered by his attentions. She is in a state of indecision and confusion, vacillating between persuading herself that a one-night stand with Bruce would be worth the risk because no one would know about it apart from themselves, and the fear that a sexual encounter with Bruce would be dangerous, foolish, and seriously damage her marriage. Anne's question for the *I Ching* is, "What are the likely consquences of a short-lived affair with Bruce?"

THE COINS	THE SCORES	THE LINES
	2 + 2 + 3 = 7	——— (line 1)
	3 + 3 + 3 = 9	—o— (line 2)
	3 + 3 + 2 = 8	— — (line 3)
	2 + 3 + 2 = 7	——— (line 4)
	3 + 2 + 2 = 7	——— (line 5)
	2 + 2 + 2 = 6	—x— (line 6)

THE HEXAGRAMS	
58 Tui ~ Happiness	*Line 2 has a score of 9 (Old Yang), and line 6 has a score of 6 (Old Yin)*
25 Wu Wang ~ Simplicity	*Line 2 changes to Young Yin and line 6 changes to Young Yang in the new hexagram*

THE ANSWER

The throws of the Chinese coins resulted in hexagram No. 58, Tui, Happiness (*see page 74*). At first, Anne took this answer as encouragement – Tui seems to confirm her own idea that passion and love can be two separate things. And after all, the hexagram confirms her own feeling that "love without affection can have moments of great enjoyment, but it is invariably transitory"and neither she nor Bruce want the liaison to be long-lasting. However, the two changing lines, line two and line six, are unequivocal in their condemnation. And because they are changing lines, they require particular attention. Line two suggests that indulging in an affair which she knows at heart is unworthy of her could lead to unhappiness and remorse. It baldly advises "Do not succumb." Line 6 indicates that temporary pleasure solves nothing and "Allowing weakness and vanity to rule... will invariably end in disaster."

In the new hexagram, line two (Old Yang) changes to Young Yin, and line six (Old Yin) changes to Young Yang. The resulting hexagram is No. 25, Wu Wang, Simplicity (*see page 58*). This hexagram is associated with "goodness," on following your heart, and being true to yourself. The "true innocence" the hexagram speaks of reminds Anne of the love she had for Terry when they were first married, when unfaithfulness would have been utterly unthinkable. Line one reminds her, too, of her first reaction to Bruce's approach – that an affair with him was simply not a good idea ("A thought that springs straight from the heart is always good; do not hesitate to follow it and carry it through"). Line four makes her think that Bruce has influenced her too much ("If you allow your judgment to be swayed by the wrong people, injury will certainly follow"). Anne must take her time and consider the situation with care – line six advises "Wait for the right moment before acting."

6TH-CENTURY VIKING BRONZE OF THE GOD TYR

ACKNOWLEDGMENTS

Key **a:** *above;* **b:** *below;* **c:** *center;* **l:** *left;* **r:** *right;* **t:** *top*

PREDICTING YOUR FUTURE

Photography: Steve Gorton

Artwork: Kuo Kang Chen *pp 45–77*

Picture Credits: **AKG London:** 31r; **Bridgeman Art Library, London/New York:** 4bl; National Museum of India, Delhi 43r; **Christie's Images:** 44tl; **E.T. Archive:** 3l; *Bergamo Carrara Academy* 1c; *British Museum* 2tc; **Mary Evans Picture Library:** 7tl, 42l, 44bl, 45tr; **Werner Forman Archive:** *National Museum of Anthropology, Mexico* 4c; *Staatens Historiska Museum, Stockholm* 80c, 30l; **Michael Holford:** *British Museum* 5br; **Images Colour Library:** 5tl; **Courtesy of the Trustees of the V&A:** 6l.

•

ELEMENTS OF PARKER'S PREDICTION PACK

Box: *Picture Credits:* **Michael Holford:** back tl;
Werner Forman Archive: *Staatens Historiska Museum, Stockholm* back tr

INSTRUCTIONS: *Photography:* Steve Gorton

DIVINATION CHOOSER WHEEL: *Picture Credits:* **Bridgeman Art Library, London/New York:** *Musea Calouste Gulbenkian;* **Werner Forman Archive**

RUNE SHEET: *Photography:* Steve Gorton

PREDICTING YOUR FUTURE JACKET: *Picture Credits:* **Mary Evans Picture Library:** back br, c; **Werner Forman Archive:** *Staatens Historiska Museum, Stockholm* back bl

Julia and Derek Parker can be contacted at their web site:
www.parkeriters.com